Consultations That Convert

How Attorneys Turn Interested Prospects Into Invested Clients

by Liz Wendling

Women & Co Press
Littleton, CO

Consultations That Convert

Copyright © 2017 by Liz Wendling

ISBN: 978-0-9846766-5-1

All rights reserved. No part of this publication may be reproduced or utilized in any form or by any means, electronic or mechanical, including photocopying, recording, or by any information storage and retrieval system, without prior written permission from the publisher.

Website: www.businessdevelopmentforattorneys.com
E-mail: liz@lizwendling.com

Printed in U.S.A.
Published by Women & Co Press
4385 South Balsam Street
Suite 11-201
Littleton, CO 80123

First Edition

Edited by Paulette K. Kinnes
Cover and interior design by Maryann Brown Sperry

Dedication

Dedicated to my family, the most significant and divine people in my life. I am blessed to have the support, love, and laughter that you bring to my life.

Acknowledgements

A special thank you to the thirty-three attorneys who graciously accepted my invitation to be interviewed for this book and for allowing me access to your practice and to your stellar intellect.

To Paulette Kinnes, my editor and now dear friend, thank you for the many phone calls and countless hours that you have put into my passion and for steering me through the book writing process so gracefully.

Table Of Contents

Foreword	xi
Chapter 1 Compelling Consultations	1
Chapter 2 Everything Starts And Ends With You	9
Chapter 3 Assessing Where Your Practice Is Right Now	13
Chapter 4 Everyone Sells Something, Even You	15
Chapter 5 Becoming An Extraordinary Rainmaker	21
Chapter 6 The Reluctant Rainmaker	25
Chapter 7 The Myths About Rainmaking	31
Chapter 8 People Always Buy You First	35
Chapter 9 Genuine Connection Is The Path To Profits	37
Chapter 10 People Skills In Action	43
Chapter 11 Showing Up And Standing Out	53
Chapter 12 How To Differentiate Yourself When You're Not That Different From Everyone Else	61
Chapter 13 Fear Of The Money Conversation	69

Chapter 14 The Client Conversion Process	73
Chapter 15 Value Is Far More Critical Than Price	81
Chapter 16 Asking For And Closing The Business	87
Chapter 17 Follow Up And Follow Through	97
Chapter 18 Erasing The Time Excuse	101
Chapter 19 The Trust Factor: Get It And Keep It	109
Chapter 20 Don't Overcome Objections, Handle Them Instead	113
Chapter 21 Networking Essentials	117
Chapter 22 Business Networking Made Easy	123
Chapter 23 Modern Marketing Methods	127
Chapter 24 Social Media Marketing: Increasing Your Visibility And Credibility	131
Chapter 25 Locking In Business Using LinkedIn	135
Chapter 26 Stop Spinning, Start Evolving	143
About The Author	149

Foreword

Consultations That Convert is insightful, encouraging, and confident. Liz's professional experience, extensive research, and natural communication skills come together in a cohesive way to help you grow your law practice. Liz has done the work to design a guidebook for lawyers so that *you* can retain more *paying* clients.

Liz streamlines the complex matters that arise from the consultations that attorneys must have with prospective clients, without trite over-simplification.

She reminds the reader, *There is no long list of bullet points that you must remember or clever acronyms that you must memorize. You won't have to use complex scripts or uncomfortable closing techniques that don't feel good to you or your client.*

The many lessons that Liz shares in *Consultations That Convert* blend in a seamless, consistent, clear, and empowering binary message: you must *change what you are doing*, and you must *be yourself*.

The examples and questions contained in the following pages will enable you to identify the elements of your client consultations that need to change. Liz also anticipated, and addresses head-on, your nagging concerns about making *any* change. She reassures the reader that *you really can choose to engage in a selling process that feels right for you at every stage*. Yep. It *is* possible.

Just last year I had the privilege of working one-on-one with Liz. During my conversations with her, Liz taught me through her words and her actions the same principles and practice tips that are packed in the pages of *Consultations That Convert*. I'll admit that *I* was initially fearful, uncomfortable, and reluctant to make changes. But Liz's words helped me to see, as I am sure they will you, the massive potential and the wonderful things on your professional horizon when you allow yourself to try refreshing and authentic ways of communicating with potential clients.

Liz, thank you for your hard work, thoughtfulness, and commitment in writing this beneficial guidebook for attorneys everywhere. I am excited for my fellow attorneys who read *Consultations That Convert*, who will then be able to *compose a natural approach that fits like a custom-made coat*.

I'm still wearing mine today, and you were right, I never want to take it off.

                    Susan Carns Curtiss, Esq.,
                    Carns Curtiss Law, PLLC
                    Founder and CEO GIRL ATTORNEY, LLC

Chapter 1
Compelling Consultations

If ever there was a time for new, it is now! The traditional techniques that enabled rainmakers to prosper in the past are no longer adequate in today's business environment. Attorneys who will excel in the new business climate are those who understand that the old ways of lead generation and conversion, networking, and sales and marketing won't work like they used to.

Business, as usual, is over. Regardless of whether you accept it, the consumer, the economy, and the business environment have changed forever. The landscape has become more competitive, sophisticated, and more technology-oriented than ever before. The old-school ways of the past have been replaced with more progressive and innovative strategies that today's sophisticated and experienced consumers not only appreciate, they also notice. If the rest of the world is evolving in response to consumers becoming more well-informed and Internet-savvy, it is in your best interests to evolve as well, or you may face extinction.

I am not suggesting that you dump and destroy every method of business development that you have ever used and start all over. But I am proposing that you scrutinize what you are doing now and see what may need a tweak, an update, an overhaul, or a burial. Take a long, hard look at your current client and business development approach.

Identifying, learning, and staying up-to-date with the right skills may turn a mediocre practice into a major contender. It's not too late to make some adjustments and catch up to what some of your competitors are already doing and profiting from. The attorneys who have evolved will tell you that a big payoff awaits when you do make these modifications and that a bundle is at stake if you don't.

This book is not about providing you with a step-by-step recipe or a one-size-fits-all formula that will guarantee your rainmaking success. Such a guarantee is not practical, nor would it be honest.

Rather, this book is about change. It is about preparing you to learn a new set of skills and concepts that will enable you to break through the boundaries of the old model of client and business development. You must have the vision, the ambition, the insight, and the intuition to not only deal with unremitting change but also to use it to your advantage to accelerate your practice and profits.

How you choose to respond in the face of change will determine your victory. If you are like the other attorneys whom I have met, you will either lean in to change or resist it.

In doing research for my third book, *The Rainmaking Mindset For Attorneys*, I discovered that today's consumers believe that you are just like your competition. They say that they can't tell you apart. Prices and fees are similar. To them, it appears that you do the same work, you provide the same information, and you have the same value and comparable expertise.

This is bad news for the legal world. But it is outstanding news for you if you are willing to implement a few changes in your practice.

Learning new and more modern ways of doing business will allow you to boost, refine, and scale your practice rapidly. Relying on business development techniques established five to seven short years ago will only get you one thing: left behind.

What worked well in the past is now antiquated, inadequate, and ineffective.

The marketplace is getting noisier and more crowded. Competition is hot on your heels, and the stakes are high. Many attorneys are competing for the same clients and the same business. To rise above the commotion, you must employ the necessary modifications that will allow you to be viewed as an attorney who has transformed along with the transformed times.

If your business development process hasn't been updated, if your sales skills haven't been refined, if your consultation approach hasn't advanced, you will miss the mark and lose clients and income.

There is no better time than now to jump out of the stands and onto the field and play the game as if your life depended on it. No matter what opponents you face or hurdles you must hop over, you are ready for it. Play the game with passion and spirit. Rainmaking is attainable for everyone. The fact that you are reading this book is a clear indication that you are ready to explore the unprecedented opportunity that is being presented to you today.

Don't think for one second that if you are remarkable at what you do, clients will beat a trail to your door and your phone will ring off the hook. Doing exceptional work alone will not prepare you for the rain. The key to becoming a spectacular rainmaker is to practice certain habits, behaviors, and skills until they become second-nature.

Just as the key to becoming a great golfer is private lessons, hitting balls on the driving range, practicing how to putt, and playing many rounds until your technique and muscle memory are developed, so it is with rainmaking for you in your practice.

Let's assume that you already have a few clients and that you do astounding work. But your practice is stuck, sluggish, or sinking. You may be spending all your time answering e-mail, filing motions, dealing with office issues, or otherwise mired in the muck. When you're in this unpleasant place, it is impossible to muster the traction that you need to build your practice.

Maybe you've noticed it happening over the past several months. Or maybe it has been happening for the last few years. Regardless, the signs are the same. Too much effort is being put in for too few results. You work hard, but your hard work isn't adding up to more income and a steady flow of ideal clients. How much longer can you keep this up?

I know the feeling. Eight years ago, *my* business was stuck, sluggish, and sinking. For three years, beginning in 2008, I struggled, but my hard work eventually paid off. I knew that it was up to me turn my business around. I had to stop doing what everyone else was doing and figure out what was right for me. I had to stop following the masses, to halt the listening to the gurus touting how easy and effortless it is to build a six-figure practice. I chose to take a giant step back and evaluate where I was. I then decided, with specific purpose, the direction in which I wanted to go.

I knew that others would think I was crazy for treading into the legal world, as I am not an attorney. But I was going to bust free on my terms, on my turf, in my own time. I knew that my choices would have a definite impact on how others would perceive me, evaluate me, and relate to me.

I am happy to report that my business went from a stuck, sluggish, and sinking business to a flourishing practice that fulfills me, not drains me. This took me stopping long enough to acknowledge what I was willing and was not willing to do. I made choices that were right for me and went for it. I changed my mindset and my skillset, and recognized my personal truth. I am now unstoppable. And you can be too.

Are you open to looking under the hood of your existing mindset as it relates to client development? Are you willing to learn the business development process that law school did not teach you? I anticipate that your answer is not only yes but hell yes!

Being a brilliant attorney only gets you a ticket to the game. A potent mindset and an updated client and business development skillset will help you win the game. Too much is at stake if you continue to come in second and watch ideal clients hire your competition. Have you tallied up the money that you are leaving on the table?

Let's consider what is at stake. Use your practice area and do some math of your own. Let's pretend that an average client means an additional $5,000 to your practice. And let's pretend that two additional clients per month choose you instead of your competition. This would net you an additional $10,000 per month, or $120,000 per year.

Now, let's also say that this increased income would not involve any extra advertising or marketing costs. You would still meet with the same number of prospective clients, but more clients would hire you because you took the time to update your approach and your consultation language so that you didn't resemble or sound like the competition. Plus, you ensured that your closing process was more streamlined and effective. You put in the same effort with a radically different result.

After doing the math, what dollar amount did you come up with? Was that number shocking? Are you okay with that kind of loss?

I wrote *Consultations That Convert How Attorneys Turn Interested Prospects Into Invested Clients* for you. You are an astute and strong attorney who is searching for the next-rung-of-the-ladder achievement, whether you are just starting out or are already wildly successful. Whether you are a sole practitioner or working in a small firm, this book is for the motivated attorney who is reaching to attain his unique, personal next rainmaking level.

Will this be easy? No way! Nothing is easy or painless on the journey to business bliss. If it was, wouldn't everyone have a booming practice and a whopping bank account? I am pretty certain that if victory was easy, word would have gotten around.

Anything worth doing and doing well takes energy. If you seek a short cut or a magic bullet to prosperity, it's not on the pages of this or any other book.

You may be wondering what I could know about working with attorneys because I am not one. This is exactly what makes me unique and how I stand out in my business and consulting practice. I have to build my practice in the same way that you do. I am responsible for bringing in clients, serving those clients, and taking care of all of the other aspects of running a business. You will have to go through the same activities and processes that I do.

I don't need to be an attorney to understand people and human behavior. I have studied the dynamics of human behavior and the psychology of sales and marketing. I know the type of trust, connection, and empathy that today's consumers expect from you. I know the language that repels them and the language that attracts them. I understand what your prospective clients need when it comes to hiring you and why they don't. I also know the type of communication and approach that influences your prospect's decision-making process and what inspires her to hire you.

I have chosen to focus my practice on designing programs for attorneys who truly want to build a thriving practice. I encourage them to step up and be audacious when marketing their services and selling themselves. I empower them to do this in a way that feels right to them and moves others to action. I show them how to internalize skills that they may use to sustain momentum toward the profitability of their practice. They become rainmakers.

I'm a cut-to-the-chase, straight-talking gal from the East Coast with a gift for simplifying complex things. I teach people real-world strategies that may be implemented right away. I don't teach an abundance of redundant, stale sales and marketing techniques; a bundle of vague clichés; or a boatload of trivial, empty closing statements. I teach the meat, the nuts and bolts, concrete ideas, solid recommendations for growing a practice.

I encourage you to read this book in its entirety. You may think that it makes sense to scan the book, skip over paragraphs, and speed-read through the chapters that you need the most, but that will be a waste of your time. You may even think: *Her ideas won't work in my practice. Been there, done that, and it failed. My practice is different.*

I am not asking you to integrate all of the ideas at once. I hope that you implement them at a pace that is realistic for you. Try one new idea. Get comfortable with it. Then try another, and another. Continue until your skills grow to a higher level of performance.

Don't expect large crowds, screaming fans, and rowdy cheerleaders! You may be doubted, your qualifications or experience deemed inadequate. Friends and family will tell you to play it safe and get a job at a prestigious firm.

Listen only to constructive people. If you do run across the people who are dream-killers and soul-suckers who want to tear you down, smile, listen, and understand where they are coming from. They are the kind of people who secretly wish that they could do what you are doing and take a risk and a leap of faith, but for whatever reason they don't do it. It may be their fears, doubts, and insecurities that they are projecting on to you.

When I began my coaching practice almost ten years ago, my golf girlfriend Alice offered me her unsolicited opinion. "My husband Ron thinks that you're crazy for starting a business in one of the worst economies on record."

Alice never missed an opportunity to inject her opinion where it didn't belong and where it was not asked for. Don't we all have a friend like that?

I did not hesitate in my reply, "Maybe Ron and I are both a little crazy because I think that he is crazy for staying in a job that he has hated for more than thirty-seven years."

I then went out into the world and built a business that flourished in the worst economy in recent memory. Who's crazy now?

If you want better results, you must make modifications and take instant and deliberate action until you get the results that you want.

The only difference between where you are right now and where you will be next year at this time is the action that you take today that drives your practice forward. When next year rolls around, what strategies will you have mastered? Will you be thriving or merely surviving? The time will pass either way.

I know it seems obvious that you need to take action. Taking action seems like the only trajectory to profits. It is.

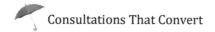

However, *thinking* about taking action is not enough. Knowing is not the equivalent of doing. Most people over-know and under-do. Knowledge doesn't produce results, action does. We all know that thinking about exercising will not make us physically fit. The best results come from action and mastery of certain skills.

Nothing will change unless you do. Nothing will change unless you apply what you read. Substantial business development habits begin with integrating ideas to fit your world, then trying them out and learning from what works, what doesn't, and how to do it better, smarter, faster, and easier the next time.

The process of applying what you learn is where you internalize and develop what works for you and then incorporate those habits into your daily activities, thus becoming more comfortable with them each time. These are the behaviors of a rainmaker.

Thank you for having trust and faith in me and for believing that this is possible. I hope that my words motivate you to embark upon a journey toward being an exemplary rainmaker. Let's leave your old way of doing business behind and move into new and bar-raising ways of growing your practice. Get as comfortable marketing, networking, and selling as you are practicing law.

Not many attorneys will have the fortitude, the patience, or the persistence to do the work that must be done to stand out and sell themselves. You do. Step onto the field. This liberating and exciting game is real, and it produces real winners. Will you be one of them?

Chapter 2
Everything Starts And Ends With You

If you want to build a self-sustaining law practice, you are going to have to take 100 percent responsibility for it. That means giving up all of your excuses, all of your victim stories, all of the reasons why you can't succeed, and all of the blaming of outside circumstances.

I will paraphrase the candid words of my first coach. *Liz, I can lay out the map and lead you to the water, but I can't push your face down into it and make you drink it. You must be willing to move into action and drink. You must be disciplined on a daily basis to achieve all that you desire. Right now you have the power, yet you fail to exercise that power.*

She was right, and I was ready. I also had the ability, as do you. You have always had the aptitude to make it, to get it right, to produce rock star results. You are now officially 100 percent responsible for everything that does or does not happen to you.

Only you know if the status quo is satisfactory or if you are ready to take the bull by the horns.

The status quo is a behavioral state where a person operates in an anxiety-neutral condition, using a limited set of behaviors to deliver a steady level of performance, usually without a sense of risk. Good is good enough. Don't rock the boat. Playing it safe is better than taking a risk.

Pack your bags, and leave the status quo behind. Nothing good happens there, anyway.

If you find yourself thinking about how your potential is being squashed and how you aspire to more, then let's shake the foundation of your practice, rattle some chains, and take some big, bold action.

Everyone has their personal status quo or comfort zone. You have built-in mechanisms that regulate your level of anxiety, fear, and discomfort. When you experience anything outside the norm, you feel anxious. Your natural tendency is to retreat into lock-down mode and crawl back inside the safety of your comfort zone.

The result of this will be that you operate into eternity in a comfortable rut that limits possibilities and earnings. If you want your practice to blossom, you have to take some risks. Deliberately push yourself out of your ruts and routines. Try things that you don't normally do. I'm not proposing cliff diving in Mexico or running with the bulls in Spain. I'm recommending that you start small, go out on a limb, expand your comfort zone, and ultimately move out to the skinny branches.

Trying new things may be scary and intimidating. Many attorneys don't want to admit that their ability to integrate new ideas, use new technology, and adapt to new strategies might require resources that they don't have, talents that they haven't tapped into, or skills that they haven't yet mastered. So what? You can learn.

Recognize that the safety of the shore may be damaging your future more than you think it is. No rescue team will magically appear and whisk you off to safety. No one is coming to save you but you. You are all you have.

It's essential that you program and develop yourself for victory. This won't happen automatically. Every day, you must choose to be the kind of attorney who expects to be victorious.

Your thoughts and your actions must be of an attorney who is programming and developing himself for wild achievement.

My favorite quote by Joanne Clancey says, *Be the kind of woman who, when your feet hit the floor each morning, the devil says, Oh, shit! She's up.*

You are in full control of what happens in your practice. Never give up your ability to control your own destiny. Success is not promised to any of us, but it is available to all of us.

Taking charge of your practice means, no more excuses. It means letting go of what didn't work in the past.

If you're having a limited amount of victory in your practice, why not try something new? Why limit your income? Why not open your life and practice up to abundance and possibilities?

Chapter 3
Assessing Where Your Practice Is Right Now

One of the greatest challenges in growing your practice is taking the time to step back from it to objectively evaluate what's going on. An assessment provides the fair and impartial vantage point needed when making pivotal decisions about the direction of your practice.

There's more to a business assessment than meets the eye. Some attorneys assume that an assessment is meant to point out what is wrong with their business. Although that's one perspective, I'd prefer that you use the assessment as a tool to identify opportunities to grow your practice rather than as a weapon against yourself.

An assessment promotes clarity, helps you to learn, and allows you to plan. It promotes the strategic use of your time and identifies areas to strengthen. As assessment provides a foundation upon which you may make keen business decisions.

Don't underestimate the value of making a brutally honest and accurate assessment of your practice. You can't begin to move, grow, and build your practice until you face reality. Avoiding self-assessment is a dangerous form of business denial, which leads to unwise and costly mistakes. A thriving practice must be built on a strong foundation. Denying any part of your present reality weakens the foundation. The truth hurts, but you can't move forward without first facing the facts.

How much do you weigh? Do you even know? Doing an assessment and looking at the current state of your practice is like stepping on the scale. If you're like many individuals, you don't want to know how much you weigh. You're happy with what you think your weight is. You avoid the scale at all costs. However, if you do step on that scale, you will know your current weight. Reality sets in, and you can no longer deny the truth.

Reality may sting, but denial is worse and much more painful. When you know the truth, you can do something about it. Many professionals don't want to look at what is because what is isn't what they want. If you want more, you must do more. Discovering that you aren't where you want to be should be emancipating. It's where the work begins.

Be truthful when evaluating the condition of your practice. Although it's natural for the always-optimistic attorney to see the current status of her business through those fabulous rose-colored glasses, it's in the best interests of your business for you to be objective so that you may get a clear picture of what is going on.

You may look at the facts and make the changes or deny the truth and play it safe. Stop telling yourself that you've only gained a few pounds and that your pants still fit. In your heart you know that you have gained fifteen pounds. Avoiding the scale doesn't change anything. You still weigh what you weigh. Denial is no longer an option.

You tell yourself that your practice is not that bad, that things will turn around, but in your heart, you know that that is denial talking. Be honest with yourself. Stop fantasizing that everything is fine or that you're busy and working hard. You know the facts.

The real delight of an assessment is the process itself. It's the time when you put your business on pause, step back from the daily grind, and objectively evaluate what your practice needs to make sure that it is headed in the right direction.

Chapter 4
Everyone Sells Something, Even You

As an attorney attempting to build a robust practice and a solid client base, you must be able to sell yourself, your ideas, and your services. But if you're like many attorneys, selling is not a natural part of your DNA. You are nowhere near as comfortable selling your services as you are delivering them. Sell doesn't have to be a negative four-letter word.

If your compensation depends upon your ability to generate revenue and close business, at some point, you will have to sell. You, and everyone else, know that sales corresponds to revenue!

In order to build your practice, you need sales. To increase profits, you need sales. To be a top rainmaker, you need sales. Sales are the lifeline of your practice. Sales are the conduit to your achievement. Victory will be arduous without profits and solid sales skills. Please digest this message, for it will serve you well on so many levels.

All of my clients would tell you that the more they embraced the sales part of their practice, the easier it got. Feel free to also call sales *lead conversion*, if you would rather. This means converting a prospect into an invested client. My clients got better at lead conversion and became more self-assured with it. The more they pushed through something that brought them anxiety, stress, or fear, the stronger and braver they became.

You know that you can never grow, never get better, never be someone who is more courageous unless you flounder through the difficult moments. Don't let fear choke off the only activity that keeps your practice breathing. One more time, it's sales skills!

One of the benefits of selling is that it offers opportunities for courage. Not many people go to their grave knowing how brave they can really be. As you make decisions throughout your day and are met with a choice, choose being daring over being fearful.

Since we're all selling something, wouldn't it make sense to learn more about it? Wouldn't it be better to remove the stigma associated with selling? Wouldn't it be optimal to get good at it?

Have you ever wondered what skills you need to add to achieve the results that you want? You can't ignore the fact that strong skills are the foundation from which you may leverage your strengths. Without proper and individualized guidance and solid skills, a practice won't survive.

You've heard the expression, *doing things the way you've always done them will get you nothing except what you already have.* If what you are doing right now was producing the results that you desired, you would already be where you want to be, wouldn't you? If your business development strategies and efforts were enough to get you the clients that you need, you would have those clients. If the way that you currently sell was enough to attract and close business, you would have no trouble building your business and increasing profits. If how you sell today isn't producing the results that you wish for, you need to transform the way that you sell.

The top rainmakers distinguish themselves from others by adopting and embracing a selling style and process that seamlessly integrates into their practice.

Based on my research and experience, most attorneys don't sell well. It's true. Why? Because they have an erroneous view of what the selling process is. Most go about it the wrong way. They believe that they have to get someone to do something that they don't want to do.

People don't like to be sold to. They never have, they probably never will. No one, including you, wants to be convinced, manipulated, or persuaded. All everyone wants is support in helping them to make the right decision for them. Treat people like the human beings they are, and watch what happens to your bottom line. Selling is not something that you *do* to someone. It is something that you do *with* someone.

Some attorneys have flat-out told me that they don't have time to learn how to sell, that selling is distasteful, or that selling themselves is unethical. I ask them how they plan to pay for office space, keep the lights on, and pay their staff and themselves? The jig is up, and they can no longer argue that they do indeed need to learn the fundamentals of selling.

There is a modern and more comfortable way to sell your expertise and your services. The old way of selling is cold and impersonal. It creates all the wrong emotions. It undermines the building of high-trust relationships. It takes way too long. And it doesn't position you for referrals. This is not the way to earn trust, get people to hire you, and motivate others to introduce you to everyone they know who meets your criteria.

Chances are that in your heart and in your gut you know that this true. You may have always been uncomfortable with some of the tactics that you have used to sell people your services, but either you didn't know what else to do, or you were doing what worked for someone else.

To stand out and sell your services, you need to choose to take part in a lead conversion process that feels right for you at every stage. Find a definition for selling that allows you to be an active and willing participant in the process.

You know in your heart and your head that by not selling your services, you can't stay in business for very long. If a sole practitioner cannot bring in business, it will only be a matter of time before his practice must be taken off of life support.

Everything you do involves some form of selling. The question is, how productive are you at converting an interested prospect into an invested client? Are you happy with your results?

Are you serving all the clients that you can handle? Are you tired of being the best-kept secret in town? Are you frustrated that model clients hire your competitors?

I have never had a single attorney yet tell me that they couldn't wait to hit the streets, pound the pavement, and sell and market their services. Not one. Clients are the lifeblood of an attorney's practice. Without clients, there is no practice and no profits.

As the old adage goes, *whatever you resist, persists*. If you resist modifying your selling strategies, you will find that resistance may be strengthening its hold. The more you fight it, the stronger it becomes.

Learning how to sell yourself first will not only change your income, it will change your practice and the way that your clients perceive you. Outstanding benefits and increased income come from knowing how to sell proficiently.

Many attorneys lose clients and opportunities as a result of stubbornness in refusing to sell. They blame the prospective client or other outside forces for the lost sale instead of asking themselves, *What could I have done better in the consultation? What I am doing that is causing someone to hire the competition instead of me?*

Attorneys stand firm in their belief that they went to law school to practice law, not spend time selling their services. Have you ever heard of the Law of Belief? This law states that whatever you believe, you will perceive. Most people have a tendency to block out any information coming into them that is at odds with their beliefs. We always act in a manner that aligns with our beliefs. If you don't believe that you have to sell, you will not sell.

Selling is getting more challenging every day. You are meeting clients who have less time, less money, and shorter attention spans than ever before.

It is harder to get your foot in the door and even harder to make your message stick in your client's mind. If you can't sell your legal services with some degree of consistency, it doesn't matter how great those services are, it won't be enough to succeed.

Dabbling in selling will produce only one thing: a long, nauseating ride on the revenue roller coaster.

Although selling legal services may be challenging, especially when the marketplace is so crowded, one of the most exciting things about it is that you have complete control. Your income, your free time, your family's quality of life, the fulfillment of your values, and the achievement of your dreams are up to you. You call the shots. You set your standards. I have never seen an attorney fail because he set his standards too high.

Below are listed some of the perks that you may expect when you know how to sell yourself and your services:

- You take control of the reins in your practice. You never fear losing clients because you know how to attract more.
- You are artful at networking events, trade shows, conferences, luncheons, and meeting new clients. You know how to cultivate personal connections with prospective clients and convert them to happy, paying clients.
- You ask for and receive good referrals. When clients trust you and are impressed with your work, they are happy to refer you to their friends, relatives, and colleagues.
- You weed out the tire-kickers and time-wasters. There will always be people who won't do business with you, but you'll find that out in an expeditious fashion and choose to let them go, resulting in amazing time savings, stress reduction, and increased confidence.
- You earn more money in less time, and it feels good to help your clients. No more feast or famine revenue cycles. You do good work for clients who appreciate your efforts.

You have the potential now to move beyond your current level of success and build your practice to exactly what you want it to be.

Chapter 5
Becoming An Extraordinary Rainmaker

A rainmaker is someone who has the skills to seal the deal and make rain in any and all conditions. Making rain and growing your book of business means that you may count on yourself to bring in business. You don't have to rely on others to ensure that you always have a steady stream of clients.

You have the freedom to build your business and grow your practice on your terms. You have the flexibility to explore new options. You decide what does and does not work for your personal practice. You navigate where you want to go.

Exceptional rainmakers are made, not born. Rainmaking is a learned skill, not an inherited trait. But rainmaking skills are not taught in law school. Making rain is synonymous with selling, marketing, and online and face-to-face networking activities.

More and more attorneys are being required to participate in sales and business development activities. Whether they work at a small firm or on their own, they are responsible for bringing in new business. This is not likely to change any time in the near future.

No matter how much attorneys know about the law, all of them who are responsible for bringing in business must learn to sell their services. This requires setting aside the old paradigm about sales and replacing it with one that serves and supports their practice.

Every professional, doctors, bankers, web designers, editors, financial planners, consultants, must learn how to sell their services. You cannot avoid the fact that you too have to sell.

Contrary to popular belief, no one personality type or gender makes a good rainmaker. No single approach makes rainmaking easier. However, a common thread ties the rainmakers whom I know and with whom I have worked together. They were bold and brave, driven and decisive, committed and consistent. They were ready to stop making excuses and start making rain. They understood how to strike business development gold.

Many attorneys carry a ton of unnecessary baggage related to the idea of sales and selling. With love and compassion, I say, get over it. Face it right now, you are the salesperson for your practice. Or if you prefer to be the lead conversion specialist in your practice, go for it.

A number of attorneys are stubborn and proclaim, *I'm not a natural-born salesperson. I don't like to sell. I didn't go into law to have to sell.*

Drop the negative energy and mindset around the only thing that keeps your practice alive and growing: sales. This negativity will no longer serve you on the pathway to profits.

Rainmaking allows you to be selective about those with whom you work. You choose to work with clients who are a perfect fit for you and your firm. No more poor-fit, pain-in-the-ass clients.

Rainmakers know that when they develop and strengthen their sales muscles, they will possess a valuable skill that many other attorneys lack.

Rainmaking for attorneys is on the rise. One of the skills that top attorneys use that convert interested prospects into invested clients is their empathy. Empathy is needed in today's selling environment. Empathy is an active force.

Empathy is the yeast of a conversation. Without yeast, the bread that you are baking falls flat. Without empathy, you may find your conversations falling flat as well. Empathy is the art of stepping into the shoes of another person, understanding their feelings and using that understanding to guide your conversation.

Build your empathy skills. Clients like it when you have empathy. It reassures them that they have picked the right attorney. Empathy is the key to emotional intelligence. It helps us connect with the other party and helps them to feel like we care about them.

Beware! Although being empathetic is one of the keys to selling legal services, this trait may also hinder your success. Too much empathy may hurt you as an attorney. If you are too empathetic, you'll say things like, *I don't want to bother you, but your invoice has not been paid. I hope that I am not imposing on you, but... I don't want to hurt your feelings... I know that you are busy, so I won't take up too much of your time...* Wipe all of these sentences off the map. Delete all of them, and anything else that resembles them, from your repertoire. They do nothing but strip you of your authority and rainmaking abilities.

Below are listed some of the attributes of rock star rainmakers:

- They do not take the word *no* personally or allow it to make them feel like a failure. The short two-letter word is just a word. Their morale is high enough so that, although they may be disappointed, they are not devastated.
- They take 100 percent responsibility for their results. Rainmakers do not blame anyone or anything else for their results. Instead, if things get worse, they work harder and become more resourceful. They look at other options and re-direct their efforts.
- Rock star rainmakers have a hunger to succeed above average ambition. These traits affect their priorities and how they spend their time on and off the job.
- Rainmakers are goal-oriented. They write down what they want to achieve and work toward their goals daily.
- They have huge amounts of tenacity, drive, and determination. They persist toward their personal aspirations no matter how tempted they are to give up.

- Rainmakers are impeccable with themselves, their word and their clients matter to them. As a result, they gain the ongoing trust and loyalty of their clients.

Chapter 6
The Reluctant Rainmaker

The number one mistake that most attorneys make in sales is avoiding it. Your ability to sell yourself and your services is directly related to the income that you earn. When you learn how to sell and convert prospects into clients, you write your own paycheck.

The best part of selling today is that you get to create your sales style. You get to be comfortable with what you say and choose the language that keeps you true to yourself. Selling becomes an extension of who you are.

Every event, meeting, and consultation that you have involves some form of selling. Many attorneys believe that they don't have to sell, so they never develop selling skills. This mindset makes their selling foundation weak and unstable, which is the main cause of not converting consultations into clients.

Let's nail this down right now. Feel this in your bones. Sales are like oxygen. You need sales to survive. Sales are how you get paid. I don't know of any other way to stay in business, besides someone handing you money for what you do, in the form of a closed sale.

To most people the word selling conjures up images of the stereotypical, obnoxious individual who won't take no for an answer, someone who uses high-pressure gimmicks and cheesy techniques to close the sale. This person lacks the fundamental ability to sell value and resorts to such tactics to compensate for the fact that he lacks the skills to spark a prospect to hire him.

Traditional, old-school sales training methods are largely to blame for having perpetuated this perception. It is imperative that you set traditional perceptions aside or erase them from your memory. When you do, you will never experience a drought in your practice again.

Sometimes selling has a stigma attached to it, and as a result, attorneys want nothing to do with it. Just like anything else, selling is a skill that must be learned, nurtured, and practiced to improve upon it. If you ignore the act of selling, you do so at your peril. Your practice won't last long if you can't bring new clients in the door.

Efficiency is the name of the game in sales. The more skilled you are, the better the return on the time that you invest.

Many of the attorneys with whom I work come to me with a love/hate relationship with sales. They love what they do, but they hate to sell. They love what they do, but they hate the process of finding new business. They love their client work, but they hate the idea that they have to sell themselves. To them, sales are a daunting and unsavory task.

Given how essential sales are to the bottom line of every practice, I am often shocked at how many attorneys would rather have a root canal than learn how to be good at selling.

The reluctant rainmaker sounds like this: *I'm not a salesperson. I don't want people to feel like I'm selling to them. I went to law school to practice law. I am not comfortable with selling. I don't want to be perceived as pushy, aggressive, salesy, or phony.*

They use these mantras as a way of letting themselves off the hook of selling. I tell them that there is another way to sell. You choose how you want to sell. Some attorneys are pushy, aggressive, salesy, and phony. And they manipulate. If that floats their boat, so be it. But you don't have to do anything that resembles offensive.

I often hear attorneys declare that they hate to sell. They believe that if they vocalize how much they hate it, they won't have to do it. That baloney only works until you run out of money, all the while proving to yourself that you don't have to sell.

Alter the meaning that you give to sales and selling, and you will alter the quality of your practice. When you shift the language or the meaning of something, it changes the emotions and feelings that you have about that particular something.

On the flip side of those power-depleting declarations, I have heard other lawyers make statements of the opposite kind. *I know that if I don't embrace selling for my business, I won't have a practice. Selling is uncomfortable for me, but I will find a way to make it fun and appreciate the process. I know that I need sales skills to grow my practice.*

If you are reluctant to sell, you are doing it wrong! Think about it. When you dislike something, do you do it well? Of course not! When you hate to do something, do you do everything you can to avoid it? Of course you do! When you hate to sell, how long do you think your practice is going to stay in business when you avoid the only thing that brings in money? If you don't sell, you are closed for business.

Some attorneys think that being good at selling means that you must be good at controlling, coercing, and convincing people to do something that they don't want to do. For them, being good at selling means that you have to be good at being confrontational. To them, being good at selling means that you have to turn into some slick-talking, money-hungry sleaze ball. That mindset is limiting your achievements and your income.

Being good at selling means that you are able to convey honesty, credibility, trust, and high value to prospects. Being good at selling means that you understand the dynamics around how people make buying decisions. Being good at selling means that you may talk about yourself and your services in a way that showcases your value and highlights your expertise. Being good at selling means that you are willing to ask for the business without breaking into a sweat, heart pounding and knees knocking. You have a choice.

Don't run out of money and run your practice into the ground by demonstrating that you're not a natural-born sales person.

You may learn the greatest skill on earth: sales. Refuse to let a fear of or a distaste for selling threaten your practice and profits. There is absolutely nothing wrong with sales pursuits. There is only something wrong with your perception of them. Every single business is sustained by sales. That means yours as well.

Suzanne, a divorce attorney who specializes in working with women and a reluctant rainmaker, hired me to virtually teach her to market her services and sell herself with self-assurance and confidence. Six years before I met her, Suzanne went through a nasty divorce, and because of this, her practice was born.

She had a great niche and utilized a nurturing, heart-centered approach in her work. Suzanne was committed to navigating her clients through difficult divorces and assisting them with their financial future. Although Suzanne had full faith in herself as an attorney and complete trust in her abilities, she grappled with fears and self-imposed beliefs about selling that kept her from operating a viable practice.

She told me that she did not want her clients to think that she was selling or pushing her services. She did not want them to think that she was only in business for the money. She thought that if she broadened awareness about her services, provided great advice, and showed her deep compassion for her clients, prospects would vault across the table, sign a retainer, and whip out their checkbook.

Suzanne avoided the entire sales and money conversation and neglected the most important part of her business: stepping up, selling her services, and asking for the business. Not surprisingly, she closed little business. Many women seeking her advice left her office with new insights and information, but few women hired Suzanne to represent them.

Suzanne suffered from anxiety and fear around asking for the sale. After Suzanne's potential clients departed her office, Suzanne felt confused, scratching her head about why she had spent hours with these prospects but never got paid for her time. Her fears and beliefs around selling cost her both time and money. She realized that she needed to change her thoughts, beliefs, and skills relating to sales. She took the leap and hired me.

I worked with Suzanne for a few months, re-inventing the experience that her clients would have when they came in for a consultation. We created a sales blueprint, new language, a fresh approach, and updated the process that she now uses with every prospect that she meets. This work helped Suzanne feel comfortable opening a dialogue to discuss her fees and services.

Suzanne is now asking for the business. She now believes at her core that she is not selling for the sake of selling. She is providing a service that assists people going through a dramatic life event and eases their sorrows and pains.

Suzanne learned that she was selling her services as well as selling her expertise, strength, trust, compassion, and ability to help other women like her. She was selling the fact that she, too, had once walked in their shoes and knew what they were going through. Suzanne turned her unpleasant divorce into a special gift. Now, she opens her arms and her practice to women who need her the most, at a time when their pain is the greatest. Suzanne is a rainmaker.

Suzanne already possessed all the knowledge and the skills necessary to practice law. She was missing the one skill that would allow her to continue to keep the doors of her practice open. You guessed it, sales skills. If you don't have them, get them. If you have the skills but they are covered in a layer of dust, blow the dust off and start fresh.

You have a choice in the story that you tell yourself. Is your story feeding your ego and keeping you stuck and safe, or is it feeding your bottom line and nourishing your soul? Serious and crafty attorneys are ready to learn the skill of selling. They are ready to refine and upgrade their sales skills and control what happens to their bottom line.

You are capable of learning a new skill. You learned how to walk and talk. You figured out how to eat with a knife and fork, read and write, dress and bathe, drive a car. You didn't decide to continue to eat with your fingers, crawl on the floor, and wear a diaper because you weren't good at growing up. You learned the skills that you needed to move to another phase of life. Now is the time to learn the sales skills that will keep your practice alive.

Tackle sales head-on, meet the challenge, and watch how your practice grows! You get to spend more time performing work that is rewarding and doing so with people with whom you enjoy working. The quicker you learn how to sell, the faster your practice will pay dividends.

Chapter 7
The Myths About Rainmaking

Of the many myths about rainmaking out there, a few of them in particular disturb me. First is that to be a rainmaker you don't need to know how to sell, rather, you should do a lot of marketing. Second, you don't need to sell, instead, solve problems, listen, help, share, serve, educate.

By the way, serving, sharing, helping, listening, educating, and problem-solving are all a part of selling. Call it whatever you want, but you are indeed selling.

Accept the fact that as a rainmaking attorney you wear many hats, and one of them must be a sales hat. You won't wear it all the time, but you will have to pop it on throughout your week if you intend to keep your practice alive. The same applies when you wear your networking hat, your marketing hat, your HR hat, your payroll hat, and your accounting hat.

There is no shortage of programs, books, and training that tout *no selling involved* or *sell without selling*. Nonsense. That's the same as proclaiming that one may go swimming without getting wet.

I know that the concept of selling without selling is alluring for attorneys who hate to sell. It is the same as someone who promises that you can eat all you want on a diet and still lose weight. This is an appealing promise for people who don't like to diet. But both of these claims are false. If marketing alone closed business, then why are so many people broke or out of business?

Selling is required if you wish to be a rainmaker. I believe that you can sell without being antagonistic. You can sell without using slimy or sleazy tactics. And you can sell without selling your soul. But it is impossible to sell without selling.

If marketing guaranteed business, you wouldn't need sales skills. All you would need to do is invest a hefty amount of money to put yourself in front of prospective clients, and the profits would roll in. Wouldn't that be nice?

Marketing is everything you do to put yourself and your practice in front of prospective clients. Selling is what turns prospects into paying clients. Marketing primes the pump. Selling makes your practice profitable.

The worst myth of all: *You don't need to sell, you just need to be authentic.*

Phrases like *just be authentic* and *just be yourself* don't tell the whole story. These catchphrases are damaging because they imply that if you are authentic, prospects will drop into your lap. If you are yourself, clients will fall in love with you and race to pull out their check book or credit card. Never! Authenticity is not enough.

That would be like me advising you not to prepare for court and know the facts of a case, just be yourself and wear your lucky red tie. I would be negating all of the knowledge and expertise that goes into winning in court.

What if being yourself or being authentic is you being a jerk? A know-it-all? Callous? A dreadful listener? Impolite? Passive?

Authenticity may be a difficult concept for people to grasp. Authenticity is an essential character trait, not just in sales, but in life. Being authentic is not a sales strategy. Everyone wants to be authentic. Of course, you must be authentic in sales. You're supposed to be authentic in business and in life! This would be like saying, *All right, universe, I am radiating authenticity, why is my practice headed for the ditch? Okay, I have been authentic all month, and I still have no clients? Why are prospects telling me that they can't afford me when I am oozing authenticity?*

Being authentic only gets you so far. Being authentic isn't enough to convert an interested prospect into an invested client. What does convert a prospective client into a paying client is a concrete understanding of the dynamics of human behavior and knowing what it takes to impact, inspire, and influence today's consumer.

Being yourself and being authentic is a marvelous way to be, but if you lack the skills to connect with others, to build high-trust relationships, and to close business, it does not matter.

Those who offer the destructive advice of *just be yourself* fail to mention the skill that is involved in driving new business. These half-truths have left attorneys with the notion that being yourself and being authentic will increase their book of business and convert prospects into clients.

Here is my authentic self, giving it to you straight. The old business development method of attracting clients is now more multi-faceted and less forgiving than ever. The competitive environment that attorneys face today is much more intense than at any time in history. It has never been more challenging to find new opportunities.

To sell well in this marketplace requires that you understand human behavior and what it takes to get prospective clients to trust you. Sales requires proficiency. Selling requires effort and technique. Sales requires a solid strategy. It is essential that you sell from an authentic place. It is vital that you live from that place as well.

When you show up as who you really are, you connect on a more intimate level with people. You're able to build more real relationships based on trust. That only helps you to be more successful, personally and professionally.

The next time that someone tells you that you don't have to sell, no selling involved, or all you need to do is be yourself, run like hell in the other direction.

Chapter 8
People Always Buy You First

People really do buy people. You could be a stellar attorney with preeminent services and an impeccable reputation, but what matters most is how clients perceive you and how you engage and communicate with them.

If you want people to trust you, and then retain you, dazzle them by taking the time to connect with them, and show them that you're a human being just like they are.

Prospective clients do not hire you solely because of your expertise. They hire you because they feel that you understand them on a level that other attorneys do not. Never underestimate the enormous value that prospects place on beginning a business relationship with someone who is sincerely focused on helping them.

Your prospective clients are buying who you are, as a unique and considerate human being first, your stellar legal intellect second. Don't hold back. Let them see the real you. Allow yourself the freedom to show off your personality and style. Showcase out your sense of humor. Demonstrate your soft side. Reveal your resilience. Display your compassion. Show your poise. Give prospects a full picture of your abilities and personality, and allow them to make the decision about working with you.

You are often the differentiating factor in a prospect's decision to buy. While fees, delivery of services, and the solution itself are significant, what makes a prospect choose you over your competitors is you.

Sales is still about people selling to people. Selling will always be about people. Somewhere along the line business became about business rather than about people. Selling is about relationships. Your best deal-closing tool is and always will be you. What sealed the deal back in the day is the same thing that seals the deal today. You! You are your greatest asset.

You are an integral part of the package. Everything you say and every move you make either pulls clients toward you or pushes them away. You either attract or repel. The way that you communicate and present yourself has a formidable effect on your credibility, your trustworthiness, and your authority.

From the moment that you begin talking, prospective clients start evaluating. Your words carry energy. Words either positively or negatively affect the impression that you are making.

Today's consumers are skeptical and don't put much trust in the words you use, so they look for other ways to gauge your trustworthiness. They assess to determine if they can see themselves retaining you. They evaluate how you make them feel and if you take the time to connect with them. You may think that prospects are buying your brilliance, your reputation, your education, your prestige, or your high-end office space. But think again. It is you, baby, all you.

For other people to buy you, you must first buy yourself. If you don't believe in yourself and what you are selling, no one else will, either. There are no tricks, gimmicks, shortcuts, or secrets. Attorneys who are the most secure and the most comfortable in their skin are those who understand that they are the largest part of the sale.

Self-assured attorneys have the ability to broadcast self-assurance, a quality that draws clients and opportunities to them. When was the last time that you evaluated yourself, your words, and the way that prospects perceive you?

Chapter 9
Genuine Connection Is The Path To Profits

Connectability equals profitability. Connection is a critical and fundamental human need. Connection creates comfort, comfort establishes trust, trust builds confidence, confidence reinforces value, and value enables people to buy. If you don't connect with others, you will not close business.

Connectability is about making someone feel as if they're the only person in the room. Every time you have a conversation with someone new, you have one primary goal, which is to make the other person feel comfortable. Your objective is not to sell them, motivate them, get them to like you, or make an unforgettable first impression.

It's easy to fall prey to the misconception that the ability to connect with others is a natural but unteachable trait, that the ability to connect is something that you were either born with or not born with. The truth is that this ability is within your control. Anyone may turn a superficial conversation into a genuine connection. Anyone may turn shallow chit-chat into a meaningful discussion.

Real connection is significant and often overlooked when meeting with prospective clients. You've most likely felt that type of connection with someone, when you walk away from a robust and generous conversation feeling lighter on your feet. You might reflect to yourself, *I feel like I have known her for years. I could have talked to him all night. It was so easy to converse with her.*

People value and pay more for the way that you connect with them and make them feel. It's hard to influence people without first making a personal connection with them. Why should they care about your input or what you think if you don't take the time to connect with them? They will tune you out. They may nod, listen a bit, but in the end, you will hear, *I have no money. I need to think about it.*

People may listen with their ears, but they make choices based on how you make them feel. Their brains are trying to connect with you, and if they do, the likelihood of them making a buying decision in your favor skyrockets. If they don't like how you make them feel, you will come in second and send another first-rate client to your competition. Don't let an additional five or ten thousand dollars go up in flames.

Have you ever given much thought to how people feel when they're interacting with you? Have you ever thought about what people experience being your presence? Are you approachable and user-friendly? Have you ever taken the time to consider whether you're truly connecting or whether you're just going through the motions?

The only assumption that people can make, and the only conclusion that their unconscious mind can form, is how relating with you makes them feel. Yes, I'm talking about the other F word: feelings. How does your presence, personal energy, and connectivity make others feel? Jill Bolte Taylor writes in her book *My Stroke of Insight, You are responsible for the energy you bring to every situation.*

We are all responsible for the personal energy that we show up with. When I say energy, I am not referring to indulging in frenetic activity or speaking with enthusiastic verve. I mean your personal and centered energy. I mean being at ease, approachable, centered, calm, focused, and open. Your personal energy relates to your connectability. This is another skill not taught in law school.

Some of my favorite skills that I teach in my practice, and some that other coaches and consultants don't, are the most potent and intoxicating of all. They are soft skills!

Soft skills are a synonym for people skills. The definition of soft skills is this: personal attributes that enable someone to interact effectively and harmoniously with other people.

You took legal courses in law school, such as contracts, torts, civil procedures, wills and trusts, property, and you may have participated in a criminal clinic. All of these courses, and more, prepared you to be an attorney. I call these the hard skills learned in law school.

Soft skills may not have been emphasized in law school. But both sets of skills are imperative for creating compelling consultations.

Now, hear this! Soft skills have nothing to do with being weak. They have nothing to do with being quiet, proper, passive, docile, spineless, well-mannered, or any other word that means the same thing.

Attorneys who have honed their people skills close more business and retain more clients. They know that it is these skills that give them the best leverage and an enormous advantage over their competition. They have a secret weapon and are not afraid to use it with precision.

Begin to notice for yourself if your soft skills need a mini repair, a modest update, or an extensive renovation.

Using soft skills means being able to transmit sincere interest, authentic compassion, bona fide connection, and heartfelt empathy to prospective clients. Attorneys with excellent soft skills are able to have an honest and open interaction with others. They are aware of what their body language communicates. Soft skills are what top attorneys use to tip the scales in their favor and produce more profits. When you embrace and master soft skills, you and your practice will never be the same. Using people skills will have an enormous impact on your practice. Those who have unbeatable people skills generally also have a high level of emotional intelligence.

Do you know someone who seems to connect with people no matter the situation? What gives them the ability to carry on dynamic conversations? What is their secret? They have superior people skills.

For many people, soft skills are often some of the hardest skills to develop, perhaps because people skills require you to get out of your logical thinking (in your head) and get into your emotional feeling (in your heart.)

Hard skills will get you an initial meeting, but your soft skills will win you the business.

Having soft skills is the new differentiator for attorneys. Don't expect anyone to mention that your people skills are smooth or that your soft skills are sophisticated. Something much more momentous is going on. Under the surface, your prospective clients will intuitively feel that something is different about you. Something about you is not like the other attorneys that they have talked to. You stand out because something is unique in the way that you interact with them.

Prospects won't be able to put their finger on or put any words to the difference. They will only know that in your presence they felt heard and seen. They may even think to themselves, *Hmmm, she is different. I feel connected. I like his style. She is sharp, and I respect her polished and professional manner. He communicates in a way that fits me. This is the right attorney for me.* Your soft skills pack a compelling emotional punch and will always serve as a strong differentiator.

I am reminded of a morning when I was leaving a meeting with a personal injury attorney.

Jonathan walked me out to the elevator. "I admire your approach. I talked to three other attorney consulting companies, and I feel like you were the only one who truly had my best interests at heart. I'm ready to learn from you and excited to have my associates work with you."

His words spoke to my heart.

Caveat #1: Be aware of what may get in the way when attempting to connect with another human being. One epic thing that keeps us from connecting with other people is our inner voice or our inner critic. We listen to that voice instead of the person that we're talking to. We're thinking about what we are going to say next while the other person is talking. We're so focused on the inner voice that we fail to hear what is being conveyed to us. The words come through loud and clear, but the meaning is lost.

Your inner critic is always asking and answering questions. *Is this true? Is this false? What's the problem? What's the solution? Should I do this? Do I like her? Do I agree? Do I oppose his views? Does this make sense? Can I see myself honing this skill? Is her proposition even possible? Do soft skills matter? I think that I am doing fine with my people skills. What's in it for me? How much longer is this going to take?*

Stop the lunacy. Pause and notice some of the exchanges that you have been having with yourself about what you're reading right now on the pages of this book. You'll hear your inner critic in action.

Your inner voice runs so constantly that you may not notice it. It has the quality of being like air to a bird or water to a fish, always present and never heeded. Listen to what your internal voice whispers. Is it constructive or destructive? If it is destructive, turn the volume way down on your inner critic.

Caveat #2: Another hidden trap that undermines your ability to seal the deal is your need to retain a new client or close the business. This trap may damage the integrity of the meeting or consultation. The ego-driven desire to win, although subtle, may also be quite dominant.

As a result, you may attempt to convince a prospect to hire you. In reality, you are trying to control the other person's decision-making process. When that happens, all of the things that everyone abhors about selling come into play: control, manipulation, pushing, forcing, and all of the other elements of outdated, traditional sales tactics. Even if you are doing this at the lowest level, any attempt to manipulate or control a client's behavior is a lose-lose proposition. This causes buying resistance on the part of the client. The more you try to convince them, the more they resist.

You may be thinking, *Aren't I meeting with this prospect because I need a new client? Aren't I supposed to try to close the business? Isn't that what the entire meeting is about?*

Yes, closing business and acquiring new clients is the optimal outcome. But wanting or trying to get the prospect as a client is inherently wanting or trying to control their behavior. This damaging zeal to *close the business* may lurk under the surface of a conversation. This mindset of wanting to secure a new client runs in the background of your head. Subtle or blatant, it is there, and a prospective client may pick up on it.

When you attempt to control someone else's behavior, they resist. This scenario plays itself out every day in typical consultations and meetings in conference rooms all across the country. Every time you try to force the closing of business, this produces pushback and resistance. If you lean in, the prospect pulls away. She may feel like you are stepping on the accelerator instead of coasting. It's astonishing how much more new business you can close when you stop pushing for it and trust the process and yourself.

Caveat #3: Another snare that we get caught in is that we think that we must change who we are when we are around different people. Good people skills are about being consistent. You are the same person with the janitor as you are with the most prominent person you know. Pay attention, and check to see if you are wearing a one social mask with one person and a different mask with another.

Like hard skills, soft skills require a lot of practice to become adept at using them. Unlike hard skills, there are no assessments to prove that you have mastered soft skills. You measure your success in developing soft skills in how well you manage your relationships with those around you, how you relate to others, how you move a prospect from being interested in you to being invested in your services.

Chapter 10
People Skills In Action

People will not trust and connect with you unless you intentionally connect with them. They will not listen to you until they feel heard first. People will not hire you unless they feel that you *get them* and take the time to understand them on a level that other attorneys are unwilling to do. Once you form a solid connection, this makes the process much more pleasing for everyone!

You will have plenty of time to talk about yourself and your services. First build that connection, and then turn it into a business relationship.

This process takes no more time than what you're doing already, but it will serve you well.

Let's review an example of two different approaches used by two divorce attorneys:

Attorney #1: Brian invites you into his office for an initial consultation.

He greets you in the lobby. "Hi, Brenda, come on back to my office. How was the traffic getting here? Is it still hot outside? Did you have any trouble parking?

"Please make yourself comfortable.

"Before we get going, I want to tell you a little about myself and how my process works. I've been a divorce attorney for twenty-two years. My firm has more than forty-four years of combined expertise. I have handled one hundred and sixty cases in the last twelve years. At this firm, we pride ourselves in treating each client with the same care and respect that we would offer to our friends and family. I have a flawless reputation. Do you have any questions for me before we talk about your case?"

Blah, blah, blah.

Attorney #2: Juliet invites you to her office for an initial consultation. She greets you in the lobby and is upbeat, open, and friendly. You notice and feel something different in her demeanor.

Juliet is focused on you. "Brenda, thank you for coming in today. I'm glad that we could meet to discuss your situation. Let's head back to my office.

"I have had a chance to read through your intake forms, and I know a bit about your current circumstances. Before we get into the specifics and the finer details, I'd like to know how you are feeling?"

Juliet allows you to share your initial thoughts.

Juliet offers her empathy. "Thank you for sharing, Brenda. I understand that initial consultations like this may feel stressful, strange, and nerve-wracking. In this office, we're not only attorneys, we're also mothers, fathers, and divorcees ourselves, so we're intimately familiar with the range of emotions, piles of paperwork, and the deluge of decisions that must be made.

"We believe that knowledge is the key to making informed decisions, so I am here to help you with some of that today. My goal is to make sure that you leave here today with the clarity and information that you need to make a decision about hiring an attorney to assist you with your divorce. Our meeting should take forty-five to sixty minutes, does that still work for you?

"Brenda, do you mind bringing me up to date on what is happening so that I may better understand how I might help you.

Then we'll discuss what it would look like to move forward and begin the process, we'll see if that makes sense at this time.

What happened?

Attorney #1: Brian instructed you to get comfortable instead of taking the time to get you comfortable. He chit-chatted about the same shallow and inane things that most other attorneys talk about. Brian attempted to bond and create rapport by asking insincere and generic questions about the weather, traffic, and parking.

He chose to begin the meeting by putting the focus on himself and his firm instead of on you. You had to wait for him to end his monologue so that you could get to a dialogue about what matters to you. Except that the monologue never turned into a real dialogue.

Brian blew it. He did not put you at ease and make you feel like you were the most important person in his day. He failed on many levels. His people skills were non-existent.

The story of Brian is an example of a typical initial client consultation, not a personal and memorable experience. At the end of the meeting the client pronounces, *I am not sure that I have the money. I need to think about it.* The client never calls back.

Attorney #2: Juliet took the time and care to design a trusting and safe environment in which honest communication could occur. She walked into the meeting relaxed and friendly. She took the time to put you at ease and allowed you to get comfortable. She eliminated all small talk and chit-chat and opened the consultation with meaningful and emotional conversation.

She used your name, twice, and wanted to know how you were feeling. Juliet made you feel like you were the most significant person that she had spoken to all day. Juliet showed you that she is caring and compassionate. She gave you the opportunity to speak first, knowing that when a prospective client talks first it may be calming and soothing.

You could tell that Juliet listened to your words. Trust and credibility was constructed quickly. Her meaningful human connection and conversation helped build your trust. Juliet showed that she was there to address your concerns and answer your questions. She made you feel comfortable enough to open up. She put her strong people skills into action.

The first thing you say to someone in a consultation is the most critical part of your exchange. Your opening comments set the tone for the rest of the conversation. It will be up to you to observe the person that you are meeting with and adjust your comments specifically to her.

Your job as an attorney is not to force someone down a one-way rhetorical street. Your job is to open every client interaction by being gentle and inquisitive. Be like water. Be open, deep, and clear.

Both of these attorneys were capable of handling your legal needs. Both had the expertise. However, only one attorney used her highly-developed people skills and her knowledge to connect with you.

My clients tell me that using their new and improved people skills is setting them apart from the competition and adding value to their clients in a way that is difficult for others to duplicate.

This is a drastically different consultation approach than most attorneys use. While other attorneys lull their prospects to sleep with their predictable opening, you must immediately show them that you are different and focused on helping them.

Think about how many times a day you have this predictable conversation with someone, *"Hi, how are you? Great. Have a nice day."*

Keep in mind that the prospect may not consciously know how or why you are different to him. His gut and intuition tell him that you are not like the other attorneys to whom he has spoken. These feelings happen on an unconscious level, which, by the way, is the level on which people make buying decisions.

Every initial meeting or consultation should open with your customized opening statement. Failing to begin a meeting with your own personal statement will result in lost opportunities and revenue. Neglecting to set the tone and intention of a meeting may lead to a meeting that goes off the rails and becomes difficult to salvage.

Top rainmakers know that in the first few moments, they never talk about themselves, their credentials, or their firm. Allow prospects to draw their conclusions about your competence and credibility by how you behave instead of by what you share. You will have plenty of time later to discuss who you are and how you can help.

As you adopt this soft-skills approach, clients will recognize your ability to understand their issues and their goals. Prospects will view you as a trusted professional who is focused on their needs and is capable of providing solutions.

One of the magnificent facets of using soft skills that makes your meetings and consultations so effective is that rather than delivering a monologue about you or your firm and the value that you bring, the client experiences your value by seeing the relationship that she will have with you. As trite as this may sound, actions do speak louder than words.

A prospect's direct experience of your value and capability is worth infinitely more than you trying to convince her with words. She does not have to conjecture or wonder about what it would be like to work with you. She feels it and sees it first-hand.

Superior people skills shift the entire dynamic of the meeting and build a phenomenal foundation for a relationship to begin. With this approach, you become a model of trustworthiness and professionalism to your prospect.

Some attorneys have pushed back against this concept. *I don't have time to hone my people skills. I'm busy, and it seems like I would have to go to a lot of trouble to learn something new. I would rather get down to business and make the best use of my time. I don't do emotions and feelings. Prospects are going to like me or not. Prospects can take me or leave me, I don't care either way.*

What these attorneys are saying is that they don't have time to pull out their people skills and have a heart-to-heart conversation. They don't have time to construct a new way of conducting an initial consultation. They are making it about themselves. These attorneys wonder why they do not stand out, sell themselves, and close more business.

This is fantastic news for you because attorneys who don't use their soft skills won't get the new business, you will. Top rainmakers know that their soft skills are the secret weapon in their arsenal. They know that this weapon goes with them on every call they make and every meeting they have.

Think of a time when a professional, such as a financial planner, a consultant, or a surgeon, awed you. What did that person do to engender a positive feeling in you? Did you sense a high degree of expertise, sincere concern for your circumstances, and a display of empathy? If so, you likely felt trust and were open and comfortable sharing information.

To achieve that level of trust, that professional had to know how to conduct a client interview/consultation. To be a rainmaker, you must do the same. Find your unique style and a communication approach that will make you stand out. Otherwise, you will blend right in with your competitors.

No matter what type of client situations you face in your practice, you need to know how to execute a persuasive and profitable initial meeting or consultation. I call this the *win or lose* interaction, the *deal or no deal* consultation. It is the conversation that spurs prospective clients to listen to you and consider hiring you or back away and head to the competition.

That means that you have to be capable of opening a high-trust dialogue, to connect and communicate, build trustworthiness and credibility, lead a discussion about the issues, ask for the business, and end the meeting on a positive note.

You may be a well-known, proficient attorney in your field and an expert on the services that you deliver, but none of that will matter if you can't master the initial meetings or consultations that you have every day.

Rainmakers who make using soft skills look the easiest work at it the hardest. Achieving a dependable level of success takes practice as well as real-world encounters. Just as you can't learn to play soccer by reading a book, you won't become adept in the essential people skills necessary to lead great client conversations without practice.

Keep in mind that the opening or beginning of the conversation is unique to every attorney. It is up to you to conceive a compelling opening that differentiates you from your competitors. It is critical that the words in the opening feel right to you and that they flow in a way that is aligned with your communication style. A tremendous opening paves the way to a favorable closing. An unproductive opening paves the way to prospects leaving your office underwhelmed, discouraged, and unwilling to hire you. The opening serves as a game-changing differentiator.

One of the elements of my practice that has become quite popular, and one that I delight in doing, is what I have termed the *Mock Consultation Evaluation*. My clients have found that conducting a simulated consultation is the most cost-effective way to pinpoint the expensive mistakes that send top-notch clients and profits to the competition. My clients realize enormous value in rehearsal and role-playing. Rehearsal is the quickest path to consultation mastery.

As a skill-boosting and growth-building tool, role-playing instills know-how and certainty and prepares attorneys to be proficient in client interactions. Evaluating a consultation is an indispensable tool that identifies skills that are weak and need urgent rehabilitation.

You wouldn't think about going to court without being sufficiently prepared. Yet, when walking into an initial consultation, many attorneys do just that. Broadway actors attend dress rehearsals to ensure that opening night is entertaining for their audience. You can do the same.

The skill of conducting a satisfactory client consultation is overlooked by most attorneys. They continue to focus much of their efforts and money on prospect or lead generation, mistakenly thinking that this will solve their declining revenue issues. It never does. Why continue to throw money at the problem of lead generation/client attraction rather than investing in the skill that converts those leads into paying clients?

Most attorneys believe that they're pretty good when it comes to their skills in the consultation. In my research I heard everything from the ridiculous to the sublime. *I suck at consultations. I'm okay, but I'm sure that I'm not perfect. I think that I'm doing all right, but I struggle with doing things all the time. My consultation skills are great, but I hate asking for the business. I do an excellent job, except for when it comes to talking about money and my fees.*

I understand that no attorney wants to admit that he doesn't know how to connect, communicate his value, discuss fees, and close a deal, but why continue to be marginal when you can be magnificent? The *Mock Consultation Evaluation* is a low-cost investment that produces a speedy return on that investment. It is what one of my clients called a *no-brainer*.

Warning: Simply changing your language as seen in the Attorney #2 example will help you to stand out. However, your words alone won't create the magic. What creates the magic is what you infuse into who you are, the feelings that you arouse in the client as you deliver your words. There is much more to the opening than what you express that will alter how your prospective client sees you. Your intention, mindset, eye contact, body language, tone, and word choices matter just as much.

I work through this crucial exercise with every client. We formulate the language, test it out, and ensure that the words come out with grace and land with ease. A fantastic opening in an initial consultation or first meeting establishes a connection, sets the tone and intention, and builds trust.

It is necessary at the beginning of a meeting to set the right tone and intention because this is the part of the meeting that elicits the most pushback and opposition from prospects, as they don't know what you intend to do to them. They think that you are going to try to close them, push things forward, and go in for the kill. They are in protection mode.

An opening statement may be crafted in dozens of ways. Make it your own. Choose your words carefully. If your statement sounds like a series of canned words coming out of your mouth, the client will hear it and feel it. If your statement sounds robotic and scripted and does not come from an authentic place, you are finished.

The language that you adopt for your practice must be easily modifiable so that it may be used in the variety of selling situations that you will face. There is no one-size-fits-all approach. Each client is so different that to expect one approach to work for every one of them is unrealistic. Initiating every meeting or consultation with one superb opening that may be modified for every situation works splendidly.

Here is a high-value bonus snippet of information. What is the one word that you can use with all of your current and prospective clients that will ensure that they notice you? What one little word can drive your business through the roof? The answer: your client's name. It is their favorite word.

Everyone loves to hear their own name. When you address your client by their name, it not only personalizes your conversation, it shows them that you are paying close attention to them. When you use your client's name, you will keep their interest. Don't overdo it, though. That makes it weird and uncomfortable.

Reflect on this old aphorism, originally spoken by Dale Carnegie, *Nothing is so sweet to a person than the sound of their name.*

When you use a client's name, you break down a lot of barriers that may block communication. You position yourself for a better relationship with your client. Plus, this helps you remember and recognize your clients. It's easier and kinder to acknowledge someone when you use his name. You don't want to blow it at the end of an engrossing conversation and have to say, *Remind me of your name again.*

Chapter 11
Showing Up And Standing Out

When you stroll into a room or a networking event, does the mood shift? Are you approachable? When you begin a client consultation, do you display anxious, needy, nervous, or self-centered energy, or are you calm, real, relaxed, and cordial? I urge you to check your energy at the door. Get a sense of what you are feeling and what you are transmitting before you step into your next meeting or consultation with a new client.

Here's why. Most people make a snap judgment in the first few moments (sometimes seconds) of meeting some new. It is human nature, and we all do it to each other. *I do like you. I don't trust you. I do feel comfortable with you. I don't see myself working with you. I do feel safe communicating with you.*

Maya Angelou sums it up beautifully and eloquently in one of my favorite quotes.

> *People will forget what you say. People will forget what you do. But people will never forget the way you made them feel.*

The mind of your prospect is subconsciously deciding whether he feels connected to you and trusts you. In the first few moments of any meeting, you connect with a person's instincts and their hard-wired responses. Subconscious survival instincts kick in, and the mind and body decide whether to run, fight, or interact. Does this person offer an opportunity or a threat? Is she a friend or a foe?

This reaction isn't based on the facts, features, and benefits that you're sharing. It has to do with how someone feels about what you're expressing. First impressions set the tone for success far more often than class, credentials, reputation, or education.

A part of the brain, the amygdala, is responsible for that hard-wired instinct. Also known as the reptilian brain, the amygdala is an almond-shaped structure in the back of the brain that is defined as the fear center. Its primary role is to process memories and emotional reactions. It is an early warning detector, perpetually checking our environment for anything that might harm us.

Your amygdala will recall if you have had a bad experience before, and these memories will be recovered and attached to what is happening in the present. The amygdala will shout at you, *Warning, you got hurt before. Be cautious. Don't trust this person. Remember what happened last time. Don't believe a word that this person says. Run for the hills.*

As an attorney, you are selling you. You are selling your expertise, your knowledge, your skills, your commitment, and your personality. Your prospect may be asking herself, *Can I see myself working with this person? Can I trust his words?* You need to find a way to connect with the prospect, on an emotional level. Communicate with the amygdala so that it will relax its defenses, and instead of filtering you out, it stops your prospect and makes her take notice. Outdated sales techniques aggravate and irritate the amygdala and send clients to the competition.

I once attended a lecture about brain science and how humans make decisions. I learned something fascinating, called limbic synchrony. Limbic synchrony is hard-wired into the human brain. Limbic synchrony is synonymous with mirroring, being in sync. We subconsciously switch our body language and posture to synchronize with the person with whom we are speaking. We sync up with that person's non-verbal behavior and signal that we are connected and engaged. We all do it.

Babies do it even before birth. Their heartbeats and body functions take on a pace that matches their mother. As adults, we do it when we are talking with someone that we like, are interested in, or agree with.

We've been unconsciously harmonizing ourselves with others since birth. Now it is time to do it consciously.

The first moments of meeting someone have a huge impact on whether they will hire you. Your verbal communication is key, but your non-verbal communication is just as critical and should not be overlooked or ignored.

Non-verbal communication refers to the communication that occurs without using spoken language. Non-verbal communication, often otherwise known as body language, is principal in getting prospective clients to listen to your recommendations and hire you.

The message that you convey in your client conversations is 55 percent non-verbal communication, 38 percent tone of voice, and only 7 percent the words that you use.

Experts recognize two levels of communication. One is conscious communication. This includes words, writing, actions, and body movements. The other is subconscious communication, which includes the feelings, or the signals, that you send to the person with whom you are communicating.

We all know and have had those feelings when we are talking to someone, and at some point we have thought: *I'm feeling a good vibe. This person makes me uneasy. I've got a good feeling about this.*

We all send out vibes and signals. When you're talking to people and meeting prospects, you may do all of the right things, but if you feel something else on a subconscious level, nothing that you do will matter to your client. The reason for this is because as the old adage goes, *It's not what you say, it's how you say it.* If your words are sending one message and your face or body language sends another, the nonverbal part of the communication will win every time.

The feelings that you have beneath the surface are infused into how you articulate something, and the person that you're talking to may feel this. People will use their gut and their intuition to make a decision, and much of that intuition is governed by what you subconsciously communicate. Don't underestimate the importance of this concept.

For example, you might verbally communicate, *I am sure that this solution will fit your needs*, but your body language indicates, *I don't know that I can pull this off.* Your words do not match what your body reveals. There is a disconnect, and others feel it. When your words and body language don't match up, you lose.

Many times others don't know how they feel, or they can't tell you why they feel indifferent about you. They only know that on a subconscious level it seems that your words and your body language are incongruent. Something is off, but they may not know what.

Attorneys who do a poor job of reading their clients may be unaware of how their body language contradicts their spoken words, since the awareness of one's body language depends on the objective feedback of others. What is your body language communicating?

One of the aspects most central to understanding what motivates people to buy is that buying is an emotional process, not an intellectual one.

Buying and selling take place on an emotional level. Feelings trigger people to buy, act, and say yes. People buy, or not buy, because of their feelings and emotions.

When you first meet a prospect during a consultation, her emotional state is often a negative one. She may be in any one of or all of these emotional states:

- Annoyed
- Scared
- Confused
- Anxious
- Stressed
- Frustrated
- Worried
- Overwhelmed

As long as a prospect is feeling any of those emotions, she is not going to hire you. In order for her to consider your services, she must feel:

- Comfortable
- Confident
- Relaxed
- Relieved
- Safe
- Protected
- Motivated
- Content
- Satisfied

This means that it is up to you to shift her emotional state. When dealing with people, you are not dealing with creatures of logic. You're dealing with creatures of emotion. Neuroscience proves that people decide emotionally and then justify their decision with logic, usually without consciously knowing it. When there is no change in emotion, the prospect has not made a decision.

Emotion always trumps logic. Realizing this is an enormous component in understanding the buyer's emotional state and then helping him to move out of it and into a different, more positive place.

How do you accomplish this? With your people skills! You ask emotional questions that put the prospect at ease. You listen and empathize. You educate the prospect and provide her with options and choices. You allow her to voice her concerns, and you respond to her objections.

Buying decisions are always the result of a variance in the consumer's emotional state. While information helps to alter that emotional state, it's the emotion that's vital, not the information. Don't undervalue the importance of emotions. Feelings are the fuel that prompt prospects to hire you.

Logic makes people think. Emotions make people act. Put another way, logic makes people need to think about it. Emotion makes people hire you. This will always be the way that people make buying decision.

Sure, logic will be a tiny part of a buying decision, but a decision to buy is primarily driven by emotion. Since nothing about buying behavior is logical, that means that you shouldn't use logic to sell. The better you get at shifting your client's emotional state, the better your results will be.

This happens every day in the dance of buying and selling. Attorneys sit down at the table to hammer out the details of a deal, armed with facts, attempting to use logic to influence the other party. They figure that by piling on the data and using reason to explain their position in the case, they can construct a solution that is simply irrefutable and get the other party to agree.

This is a recipe for disaster because decision-making isn't logical, it's emotional. You must take the time to tune in and turn on the emotions in your prospect.

Attorneys who don't feel their own emotions will never touch their clients' emotions. But a keen attorney knows that people buy emotionally, and they are willing to go there with a prospective client. Emotion is what drives a prospect's buying decision.

Some attorneys will argue this point to the death because they're uncomfortable with the notion that they must access prospects' emotions. Like it or not, that's the way it is. It's reality. Arguing with reality prevents attorneys from earning a sizable income. Deliberating on this concept drives my attorney clients crazy because they spend so much of their day in logical thinking that they have to consciously move from their head to their heart. I tell my clients that the journey is a short one. It is eighteen inches from the head to the heart. I encourage you to take the trip from logic to emotion.

If you don't like the word emotion, replace it with chemistry. If you do not develop chemistry with your prospective client, there likely will be no client and no new business.

Think about when you may have gone on a date or two and then come to a conclusion. *We did not have good chemistry.* This happens both personally and professionally.

Feeling chemistry is critical in your prospect's decision-making process. Some people are naturals at effortlessly putting people at ease. They have an innate ability to detect authentic harmony and get people to open up and feel comfortable with them. Others are not so lucky and have to work at it.

By now, you should know if you connect with people easily or if it takes you a bit more time. Either way is okay. There is no wrong way here. Just make sure that you get this concept.

Still not convinced? Are clients and opportunities disappearing before your eyes? You know what I mean. You may have thought that a prospect was guaranteed to hire you or choose your firm, but he slipped through your fingers at the last second. Perhaps you found yourself working on a promising opportunity when suddenly, with no explanation, the opportunity spins out of control and is lost?

You're certain that you have connected and communicated with the prospect. You clarified everything that your prospect needed to know about your services, and she has a sufficient budget. You tell yourself that it's in the bag and high-five yourself in your mind.

Then out of nowhere, you hear something like, *I liked you and will give it some thought. Your presentation was incredible. We'll keep you in the loop. What you have shared makes a lot of sense. Let me run it by the others. I need to think about it, and I'll get back to you.*

Why does this happen? You may have attempted to inspire someone to buy from you using logic, not emotion. Logic cuts off possibility. Emotion opens up opportunity.

You may be the best and brightest attorney in the world. You may make every rational argument to demonstrate why it makes sense for someone to do business with you, but if you don't appeal to your prospects on an emotional level, you're just another person trying to sell them something.

Chapter 12
How To Differentiate Yourself When You're Not That Different From Everyone Else

When it comes to the present, one thing is certain. Your prospective clients are on the hunt for an attorney who is choosing to utilize a fresh approach and explore innovative ways to stand out in the sea of legal competition.

A major danger to your practice right now is not being able to define what sets you apart in a world that is cluttered, competitive, and crowded.

These days it is not enough to be a brilliant attorney. It is not sufficient to provide an excellent service. Today you also must have additional assets. Have you identified your edge? What sets you apart from your competitors? What value do you provide, and how is it different than the alternatives?

The competitive environment that attorneys face today is much more intense than in the past. It has never been more challenging to find new business. The changes are so significant that your practice won't survive without differentiation.

If you choose to stay where you are and continue to look and sound like your competition, you are making a conscious choice to languish in irrelevance.

It takes a winning combination of attitude, commitment, knowledge, skills, and talent to stand out in this fast-changing and highly-competitive environment.

Remember when acquiring new clients was easy? Referrals drove the growth of your practice? New clients fell in your lap at the right time. That is now a thing of the past. Referrals may still come in, but the once-steady flow is slowing down to a trickle. Why?

- Lack of differentiation ~ you are being seen as a commodity.
- Heightened Internet savviness ~ clients are deft, fast, and better informed.
- Diverse types of competition ~ online and do-it-yourself legal solutions are the trend.

To gain a substantial advantage, you must be different from your competitors, and different in a way that makes a difference to your prospective client. Otherwise, you will fall head first into the commodity trap.

How do you escape that commodity trap? Some attorneys complain that clients view their services as a commodity, leading them to ask for discounted fees. If clients indicate that they can't differentiate your services from those of others, what they're vocalizing is that they can't see that what you deliver is different than what your competitors offer.

Now the commodity game begins and shifts the competitive encounter to something that people may differentiate: your fees. You may escape the commodity trap with the ideas and the value proposition that you present to the client. Differentiate yourself from your competition by demonstrating to your prospective client that you bring more to the table than your competitor, more than simply legal services.

Every attorney and every practice area bring something different to the value table. The burden of proof is on you. You can't count on prospects to recognize on their own the value that you bring to the table, to calculate what your services are worth, or determine if they should pay your fees.

Many attorneys have a tough time answering these questions: How do you stand out from your competition? How are your services different than the last firm that I retained? Why should I hire you instead of the firm down the street?

Some declare that what differentiates them is where they went to law school. Others proclaim that it is how long they have been practicing. Some think that it is the prestigious firms where they have worked. Some assert that it comes down to their mission, vision, and values. All of these mundane things are now monotonously pontificated about on countless websites and blogs.

Some attorneys answer the *how are you different* question like this:

- I have been an attorney for more than twenty-three years and have an outstanding reputation in family law.
- I am proud of my practice and the outstanding services that I provide to all of my clients, during what may be an emotionally challenging time.
- I listen to you and understand your needs.

Prospective clients have also heard this: *Our firm opened in 1966, and since that time, we have been the best provider of patent work in this area. Our staff is knowledgeable and experienced. Our fees are competitive, and we pride ourselves on the service that we deliver to our clients.*

What the prospective client hears is an advertisement about how great you are, not how what you do delivers value to him. Your answer is stock and standard...and generic and boring. It is outdated and old-school.

After reading or hearing these statements, how do you feel? Interested in hiring one of these attorneys? Excited to retain the services of one of them? Hardly. In fact, none of these attorneys have told you anything that you didn't already expect to hear! You've probably heard it all before, from countless other attorneys or their websites.

At this point, the prospect has no way of differentiating one attorney from another, except a gut feeling and, you guessed it, price. Distinguishing your services from those of your competitors will result in wins for you. Failure to differentiate yourself results in an apples-to-apples comparison. The attorney with the lowest fee gets the business.

With a re-phrasing of two words, any company, anywhere in the world, on any website, may announce the same thing. *Our auto body shop opened in 1966, and since that time, it has been the best provider of auto repair services in this area. Our staff is knowledgeable and experienced. Our fees are competitive, and we pride ourselves on the service that we deliver to our customers.*

It is often only this lack of differentiation that makes clients shop price. Your fees may be the only difference that prospective clients see.

Other attorneys answer the *how are you different* question this way:

- We have decades of experience that you can trust.
- We provide one-on-one attention to all of our clients.
- We are committed to long-term relationships.
- We are dedicated and loyal.
- We treat every client with care and respect.
- Our attorneys pay special attention to fine details.
- Our expertise is the best in the state.
- We care about your financial future.
- We will walk you through every step of the process.
- We protect what's most important to you.
- We take the time to listen to your needs.
- We put our clients first.
- You are number one in our eyes.

Statements of this kind are also splashed in bold letters on attorneys' websites the world over.

Meanwhile, clients are thinking, *Damn, I was looking for an attorney who is unethical, a poor listener, misses commitments, is not dedicated, places me second, lacks attention to detail, and has little experience.*

Your affirmations about how you are different are irrelevant to prospective clients. Using statements that are predictable, over-used, and unoriginal is not differentiating yourself.

None of the above statements offers a whiff of uniqueness. These declarations cause you to blend in with your competitors. They do nothing to make you stand out. They do nothing to set you apart. They do nothing to highlight what makes you special. Every single one of them is a baseline expectation for prospective clients.

Let's imagine that a prospect asks you why you are different, perhaps in the middle of a consultation. She is not asking for the answers that you typically give. It is a bit of a trick question. She is looking for how what you do differently affects her. She wants to know it relates to her, how it adds value to her, what it means to her personally.

I will give you an example here, but I urge you to put some thought into the statements that you make about how you're different.

I teach my clients how to differentiate themselves by using language that the client has already shared and loop it back to him.

If a prospect asked me, *Liz, why should we hire you as a consultant? Why should we have you train our attorneys rather than any other consultant out there? Why are you different?*

He might expect me to proclaim, *I am the best in the industry. I deliver outstanding results with my programs. I can double or triple your practice revenue. I have been in business for ten years. I listen, I care, I make my clients a priority.*

These over-used claims would be generic and expected. These basic and boring statements don't cause someone to see me as exceptional and outstanding.

Instead I might state, *Richard, that's a valid question. I know that my competition does a few things the same as I do. However, my style and systems are quite different. Earlier you mentioned that you were not at all interested in investing in an off-the-shelf or generic one-size-fits-all program for your attorneys. You wanted to invest in something new, fresh, and updated. You wanted something that would help your attorneys convert more consultations into clients.*

My consulting is distinctive because I not only teach attorneys how to sell themselves and their expertise, I invest additional time is helping them understand the psychology around why people buy and what they need to make buying decisions. This leads to converting more interested prospects into pleased, paying clients.

Richard, you also mentioned that you don't like to use word-for-word scripts that sound robotic. Some other consultants lean heavily on using generic scripts that work in many industries, but unfortunately, generic scripts make it much harder to stand out. I customize the process and utilize language that fits your attorneys and the culture of your firm. I don't believe in cookie cutter, one-size-fits-all language.

Then I stop and check the prospect's understanding. *Richard, is that correct? Did I get that right?*

Pause, take notice, and see where this is going. I tied the question of how I am different back to something that the prospect told me in our initial consultation.

Richard may reply, *Yes, you hit the nail on the head. We don't want to use a generic script. We have to do something different to stand out. The competition is growing, and coming in second will not cut it anymore.*

I know that I did not respond in the way that Richard expected. My answer was what he needed and valued hearing. People don't want me to launch into a speech about how great I am and all the wonderful things that I can do. I handled the *how are you different* question by addressing the concerns that Richard shared with me throughout our meeting. I answered the *how are you different* by being different.

Shifting your approach will not only make you stand out, but it will also increase your bottom line. It did for me. I know that I win more business because I know how to be distinct. I know that that distinction serves as value, credibility, and a trust-builder.

Please do not dispatch a canned, insincere, and unoriginal response. The attorneys to whom I have taught this concept tell me how refreshing it is to answer the *how are you different* question in a way that doesn't make them justify or validate who they are. This approach has tremendous value for them.

The more that your language caters to what's in it for the prospect, the more successful you will be at grabbing his attention and gaining his interest. It *is* all about him, it is not about you.

Prospective clients filter your words through their perspective. Think about how you plan to articulate important information about you, your service, your firm, and how you are different. Prospects need to hear you and feel what you say.

You don't want to sound like every other attorney. Take the time to drill down and develop a message that sets you apart.

Do the following exercise, and give this critical aspect of your practice some consideration. Spend time thinking about what makes you distinct. Ask others what they think makes you unique. Everyone has a differentiator, so don't let yourself off the hook until you discover yours.

Below are some questions to ask yourself:
- What is my unique offering to the marketplace?
- What are my distinct characteristics, quirks, areas of expertise, skills, and attributes?
- What is the look and feel of my brand?
- How can I integrate that uniqueness into all of my messages, promotional materials, writings, speaking engagements, and services?
- Once defined, how can I make my singular traits recognizable in a stable and sustainable way?
- Who is my biggest competition?
- How is what I do different from what the competition does?
- Who do I know that may give my firm and me an advantage in the marketplace?

Define your difference now. Not later, now! Not when you get around to it, now! Not when you're in the mood, now! Not when your plate isn't so full, now! Not when your schedule clears, now!

Chapter 13
Fear Of The Money Conversation

If there is an aspect of selling that makes you uncomfortable, you may subconsciously try to avoid doing it or only do it to the point of comfort. All human beings do this.

Mastery of any process requires you to be as conscious as you can about what you are doing. The greater the consciousness, the greater the mastery. You must face the fear, not turn away from it.

More than three-quarters of my clients have some resistance or fear around talking about money or fees. I tell them that discussing money and fees needs to be like breathing. It has to happen without you thinking about it. Money needs to be a straightforward element of every conversation.

When it comes to selling yourself and your services, many of the actions and behaviors that you were taught when you were younger become counterintuitive. Messages like *don't talk to strangers* and *never talk about money* may linger in the back of your unconscious mind. You must make a deliberate effort to accept that your behavior needs to change if you wish to build your book of business. You must re-program your past perceptions of what is, and is not, acceptable in a sales environment.

Failure to have the money conversation with a prospective client put doubts in the client's mind. It's not logical and raises suspicion when you avoid the money and fees conversation.

Reluctance to discuss fees at the beginning of a relationship may lead to awkward money conversations down the road. This includes the uncomfortable money conversation wherein you have to inquire, remind, and nudge clients to pay you. Get used to bounced checks and sob stories, all because you resisted having a straightforward money conversation out of the gate.

If you resist talking about money, your client will have resistance about paying you money. Just like a magnet, two parties with money issues find each other.

Rarely do clients come out and tell you when you did something that caused them to take their business elsewhere.

Patty, an estate planning attorney, called me after realizing her precarious position. *"I need your help. I get weird when I talk about my fees and how I get paid. If I don't address this issue now, I will continue to lose business."*

Patty informed me that a prospective client had come right out and told her that she sensed her awkwardness talking about her fees.

The prospect stated, "If you are uneasy discussing money, I know that I will be uneasy about you handling mine."

I know that talking about fees and money may be awkward, but there is no way around it. Part of my coaching work is to help my clients fashion their own unique and strategic money-talk for their practice. I teach them to discuss their fees and explain how they get paid in a way that puts them and their client at ease. I show them how to clarify how their fees are paid, how the money will be used, and what happens when invoices are outstanding. This conversation is fair and firm and comfortable and confident.

You tell the client, *Here are the details about how I get paid for my work!* When you position money-talk as a candid and straightforward conversation, no misunderstanding occurs about your fees and how you are compensated for your time and efforts.

You must personalize and customize a money-talk that matches your personality. I enjoy teaching attorneys how to craft their customized language related to money and do this in a way that is comfortable for them and stirs a positive response in the client.

When you drop the resistance and lose the fear around talking about money, something miraculous happens. You get paid for your work. Shocking, right? Clients appreciate and respect attorneys who take a professional approach to the money discussion. Smart rainmakers know that stepping into a strong money conversation sets them up for advancement. If you feel like you are chasing money, your clients are dragging out payments, invoices are outstanding, and you are working for a client who is not paying you, stop the madness. Fix this issue without delay. This open money wound will never heal itself.

I listen to many attorneys blame their clients for unpaid invoices. They are shocked when a client does not bring his account current for sixty to ninety days, or even longer. They get upset that they are doing the work and feel that their clients are being disrespectful. They play the victim rather than the victor.

I tell these attorneys that they are setting themselves up for this scenario every time they deliver a half-hearted and weak-willed money conversation. They are responsible for the client's behavior because they voluntarily evaded the money conversation.

Non-payment will continue until you step into the money-talk with ease, grace, and poise. Eliminating the fear of the money-talk won't happen overnight, but in time, with persistence and perseverance, it will happen.

Chapter 14
The Client Conversion Process

Every attorney uses a process, day after day, consciously and unconsciously. In sales, your success, or lack thereof, is always obvious. Either you succeed in bringing in business and hitting your revenue goals or you don't. Only you know if your process is working for you. Only you know if it is draining you or fulfilling you.

If you googled the term *sales* or *lead conversion process*, you would get more than nine million results. From those results, a dizzying array of ideas, mechanisms, and approaches would hit you between the eyes.

While countless suggestions are available to choose from, I have found that my eight-step process works for most attorneys and aligns nicely with the buying process of most prospects. It is optimal for attorneys who conduct free initial consultations. It is easy to execute and has a sequential natural flow.

Your task is to coordinate your sales process and your prospective client's buying process. We all have a process that we use to help us make decisions. Buying decisions vary from person to person. Some people make decisions quickly. Others ponder and deliberate forever to come to a decision.

I make decisions swiftly, rarely change my mind, and do not generally suffer from buyer's remorse. I know what I want, and if it feels right, I buy. Others contemplate, meditate, and ruminate about whether to commit to a yes or no. Some research for weeks or months. Some will never make a decision. To them, making no decision is a decision.

It is reasonable to inquire how a prospect makes decisions. *What process do you go through when making decisions? Now that you have the information, how long will you need to make a final decision? What is your timeframe for making a decision to move forward?*

When I am working with my clients on their process, we dive deep into each step in detail. As you will see below, each part of the process has its own language and set of skills. By understanding each element and creating a customized approach to selling and lead conversion, you close more business. The speed with which you implement your new process is directly related to the speed in which you see results.

The process is unique to every attorney. Every attorney should have the ingenuity to let her individual personality shine forth while selling. Once complete, attorneys may use their new process over and over for years to come. Their process speeds up the learning curve to greater accomplishment. However, we may adjust things down the road to account for shifts in the marketplace, technology, and other things that may come up.

Having a process that is unique to you and your style is key in differentiating yourself in the marketplace. It is impossible to sound like every other attorney because you and I will shape your exclusive system and customized approach.

A pastry chef has a process for baking a pie, a Super Bowl quarterback has a process for throwing the football, an artist has a process for painting a picture, and an attorney must have a process for creating an incredible client experience. Anyone who is successful has an identifiable process behind that success.

A process takes the pressure off of you and puts the primary focus on your client. When you have a process, you can relax and be cool. Rather than focusing on yourself and worrying about screwing up, you are now at ease and focused on one thing, your prospective client.

A process delivers predictable and reliable results. When a process is effective, you know why it works. When you can predict a result, you will be thrilled to repeat it over and over, which will lead to more closed business.

The textbook definition of a sales process is a structured, systematic, logical, and documented step-by-step approach to selling a product or service where a progression of defined steps is followed and results in the completion of a sale. My modified definition of a sales process is a set of structured and defined steps that effectively move an interested client into an invested client and a raving fan.

A sales process is not robotic or inflexible. If you feel opposition toward this dynamic tool, this chapter is for you. Don't underestimate the vitality hidden in this tool until you fully understand the impact that it will have on your practice.

A sales process is the road map that facilitates your ability to close more sales in a shorter period of time. All attorneys should clamor to use this tool. It is a must-have in your firm's tool box.

Many attorneys would rather go with the flow and take a chance that they will be able to seal the deal. Their process is not structured or logical, it's scattered and inefficient and produces poor results. Or they have one or two skills in their tool box and get lucky now and then.

Mastering one or two skills alone won't generate the same results as understanding and mastering the entire process. There are parts and pieces to every process, and some of them are distinctive for every practice. But the capacity of the tool is not fully realized until you use all of the parts and pieces together. Understanding and applying the principles of the entire process leaves nothing to chance.

The word process comes from the Latin word procedure, which means to proceed, and is a series of operations or stages that lead to a specific outcome. Regardless of what you sell, the process is like a production line, and it follows a certain sequence. Every sale is the result of a series of regular behaviors and actions.

There are many moving parts to the process: building chemistry and making a connection, inspiring trust, asking questions, talking about fees and budgets, handling objections, securing the business, and consummating the sale.

One size does not fit all. You need a custom process to ensure the potency and efficiency of your practice. Designing sales processes is one of my favorite things to do for attorneys because the rewards that they may reap are so tangible in this task. The return on investment is monumental.

The Eight-Step Sales Process

The following step-by-step approach will help you forge a stronger case for your services and expertise without hard selling and leads to a more stress-free close.

Even though the conversation is loosely structured, it permits an intuitive, authentic, and natural conversational flow. Please know that there are many other nuances to every sales process. I customize the process to each client based on their personality, practice, and style.

Below I have given you a framework to use so that you may begin to customize your sales process.

Step 1: Connect, Open Up, And Build Rapport

Your goal is to stimulate trust by intentionally connecting with your client. Ask questions. Get in her world. Forego the temptation to talk about yourself and go into monologue mode. Make her feel as if she is the most essential person that you will talk to all week. Resist talking about obvious topics such as the weather, the traffic, the parking. Let all of the other attorneys out there bore their clients with those humdrum, outdated conversation starters. Use your imagination. Make it about her.

Step 2: Ask The Prospect To Share With You

Get permission to get personal about what is going on in the prospect's life. Be curious with him. Let him know that you're going to ask questions so that you may better understand his needs and what solution will be most helpful to him. Tell him that the only way to see if you are a good fit is to dive into the details of his problem. You want to make sure that you understand the key factors driving his decision to seek your counsel.

Step 3: Needs Analysis

It is here that you must ask deeper questions, uncover needs, and find out what is going on in a prospect's world. This is not the time to go off on a tangent about your services and how long you've been practicing law. Why? Because the prospect is not in listening mode yet. She is in talking mode. At this point, she needs to be heard.

This step is about strengthening credibility, not by talking about yourself and what you offer but by demonstrating your listening skills and your business approach. The spotlight should continue to shine on the prospective client.

Step 4: Listen And Probe Deeper

This is where some attorneys miss the mark. They are so concerned about what to say and how to say it that they don't they don't dig deep enough. When you ask intelligent and purposeful questions, you go from simply being some random attorney to being a trusted resource and an expert in the client's eyes. He understands that you know what you're doing and that you're there to listen to and help him.

More in depth questions allow you to uncover information and discover the truth. Questions will help you determine if and how you may assist the client. Questions give you immense insight into the way that it is best for you to present your services as solutions to the prospect's problems.

Step 5: Summarize And Prioritize

Summarize what the client has shared with you so that she knows that you understand her situation. The summary should take sixty to ninety seconds and will ensure that both you and your client are moving in the same direction. Clients appreciate when you mirror back to them what they have articulated to you because it proves to them that you were paying attention. Use the exact words and language that she used when answering your questions. This step further increases your credibility and value and gets the client geared up to talk about solutions.

Step 6: Collaborate To Find Solutions, And Handle Objections

You've assessed the opportunity, and now it's time to discuss options and solutions. Now it is your time. Instead of jetting into selling mode, here is your chance to present your services before you make an official offer or proposal. Instead of making one suggestion, hone in and find the right solution together. Brainstorm. This will entice the client and allow him to determine what it is that he needs and conclude that you're the person to provide it.

You may encounter an objection or two in this step. Objections are part of sales and business and will never go away. But objections are nothing to fear or avoid. View the objection as a request for more information or as a prospect's concern. Every objection provides you with a new opportunity to share the right information with a prospect and to move him into the next step of your sales process.

Step 7: Asking For The Business Or Next Steps

It's closing time. Unless you complete this step, you're not done. Closing is the logical conclusion to an effective client conversation. Closing is the natural occurrence when you have completed the first six steps of the sales process. It is in the close where your efforts are rewarded.

You have the obligation to ask your client for some type of commitment. This looks different with each individual client, and you must keep the momentum going.

But let's assume for a moment that a decision has not been made and that the sale is not closed. If this is the case, do not skip this step. This is where everything could fall apart. Before ending a meeting, agree on a specific next step. This is an agreement to take a specific action within a specific time frame.

Many attorneys lose control of the process and end a meeting or consultation without an agreed-upon next step and no plan for future action. Who will contact whom? When? The prospect might face you as she prepares to walk out the door. *Thanks for your time, I will let you know.* Or you fumble through a banal closing statement. *Well...let me know when you're ready.* But no specific next step or timeframe for what will happen when has been decided.

It is your responsibility to keep the ball in play by making a plan for the next step. You lay the groundwork. *This is what I propose for our next step. Why don't we schedule a date and time to meet so that we may discuss the best way to proceed.*

This ensures that you leave every meeting knowing what will happen next. Never depart without knowing what the next step will be for all parties involved.

Step 8: Follow-Up

When it comes to follow-up, do you do what you say you will do, when you say that you will do it? This is not the time to drop the ball. Follow-up is within your control. A good follow-up system will keep sales moving and keep your business in business. Clients respect efficient, organized, and dedicated attorneys who follow through. When you follow up, you win clients.

So there you have it. A process gives you definable steps, predictable outcomes, and measurable results. Keep in mind that different components of this process may be used in a wide variety of situations. It is up to you to determine the most appropriate elements of the process to be used in a given set of circumstances.

In using this process, it may take an hour to gain a new client. It may take as many as three years. This all depends on need, time, budget, urgency, and other factors. The essential thing to learn is that you must employ a process. Don't rely on the expensive, winging-it method of winning business.

This process may be different from what you have always been taught and different from what we think would be effective. Yet my experience, together with feedback from clients, has shown me conclusively that consultations and meeting are more productive and gratifying and lead to a significantly greater number of new client relationships when this eight-step process is used.

Chapter 15
Value Is Far More Critical Than Price

Adding value to your legal services is an absolute necessity. To separate yourself from competitive options, you must create an environment in which the prospect may see the value and the expertise that you provide. If your prospects can't otherwise discern value, they are going to use the one measure that makes sense to them, your fees.

The concept of delivering value is one of those things that is both simple and complex. It is simple because delivering value does not have to be grand or costly. It is complex because it may only be identified by the client, because different people place significance on different things and to different extents.

What's valuable to one person might not be prized by another. Things are only valuable if they are valuable to that particular client. What you think you are worth and what others think you are worth may not be the same. What you think is meaningful and valuable may not in any way be consequential to your client.

If a client informs you that she is going with a competitor who has lower fees, she is telling you that she does not see enough difference in the things that are of value to her to substantiate the difference in price. This is no different than buying a new computer, an appliance, boots, or home furnishings. If all of the choices appear to be the same, why would someone pay more?

Did you really lose the sale and the opportunity because of your fees? Let's first address the issue of when it really is about the money. If your prospect does not have sufficient funds to hire you and does not have the financial means to pay your fees, then yes, that is a money issue. There will always be people who cannot afford your services.

However, if your prospect has the financial ability to hire you, this eliminates price as a reason for choosing your competitor. If he has the funds to hire you but chooses not to do so, then money is not the issue that is driving his buying decision. Value is the underlying driver.

So why did you lose the client and the opportunity? You lost it because, after weighing both options, the prospect did not see enough difference in value between your services and your competitor's to justify spending the additional fees. This has nothing to do with your fees. It has everything to do with your failure to differentiate your value proposition.

When selling against competition, your success depends entirely upon your ability to demonstrate that what you have, in terms of value, is superior to the other options being contemplated. Differentiating yourself and your services from those of your competitors will result in steady wins.

In the absence of value, virtually any product or service may be driven down to one thing, price. If you deliver value, you will never have to compete on price. Don't allow price to become a default position. Don't allow your fees to be the only point of reference available for separating one option from another.

It is your obligation to the potential client to help her make a well-informed decision by showing her your value.

Value is the difference between the fees that you charge and the benefits that your prospect perceives that she will get. If your prospective client perceives that she will derive an outstanding benefit for the price that she pays, then her perception of value is high. You control the dial on this perception of value. The more you focus on the value that you deliver, the less important price becomes to the prospect.

When you add value, you provide the prospect with something that he is not expecting. You offer him something that makes him view you as distinct, not like all the others. It is up to you to know the value that you bring and what is valuable to your clients and speak to it.

Value is in the eye of the beholder. No matter what you believe about the value of your services, it is the client who decides the value that you provide. The client is the final arbiter of value.

Given the competitive nature of business, how do you separate yourself from all of the other options? How do you show a prospect, clearly and conclusively, that you are not like other attorneys from whom they may choose? How do you provide the type of value that would make a prospective client pay higher fees for your expertise?

Showcasing value is accomplished by how you position yourself and the type of questions that you ask. The questions that you ask and the way that you ask them will allow the client to step back and see her situation from a different perspective. The client is likely to gain new insights and understanding about the obstacles that she needs to deal with.

You tip the value scales in your favor because you are the trusted advisor who helped the prospect gain a different perspective. You shined the light on something that he did not realize or think about.

You silently communicate to the prospect, *Whether we end up working together, you will get value from our interaction. You will leave here today with something to think about, something that piqued interest, something that jostled the status quo.*

It is a common fallacy that people buy based on fees or price. Some do, of course, but most people buy based on value or their perception of value. Some attorneys open their practice with the thought that they will enter the market and simply offer what they have at a lower price and their business will do fine. They soon see how false this is.

Prospective clients are afraid to part with their money. Money equates to security, and it doesn't matter whether you're asking them to part with $195 or $1,995. People are happy to spend their money when they see that there is more value in using your services than there is in keeping their money.

In nearly every buying situation, the prospective client visualizes an imaginary set of scales or balances in her mind. In the decision-making process, the prospect uses those scales to weigh the value of the product or service being examined. What happens in too many cases is that attorneys do a lousy job of presenting the specific benefits and value of the service that they offer. They fail to show the client how she will be much better off after hiring them or procuring their services.

When this happens, the value of what you deliver and bring to the table is not seen. Your clients get their value scales out and determine the benefits that they would receive versus the money that they would be required to spend.

This is the moment where the weighing game begins in your client's mind. He is weighing to see if value does exceed your fees and the benefits outweigh the cost. If so, you win the business. If not, you start all over with another prospect.

If the prospective client feels that what you describe is what she thinks she can get from a less expensive attorney or online legal services, she will not retain you. She perceives the value in your offering as just like the guy down the street, or worse, the same as an online legal service such as LegalZoom.

People don't always buy based on the lowest price. No one believes that the lowest price ever equals the best quality. You don't win clients, opportunities, and business on price. You win them on the value that you create. If price was the only thing that mattered, and people were looking for the least expensive options, everyone would drive a Kia, Nordstrom would be void of customers, flying first-class would not exist, and we would all drink Folgers coffee.

Selling on price alone is a losing proposition. Show prospects the value in what you offer, and many price objections will disappear.

It is important to understand what your clients value before you can give it to them.

Did you think that this was going to be easy? Figuring out this value stuff is hard, and there is no one right answer for everyone at all times.

To sum up what value means, take the time to find out what your clients value and give it to them. But don't stop there. Give them some of what they didn't even know they wanted. It's the extra little kick that leaves clients with that WOW feeling.

Chapter 16
Asking For And Closing The Business

Asking for and closing the business is the hardest, most avoided component of the sales process, and the most frightening. Attorneys know that they need to ask, but the fear of asking stops them dead in their tracks. It's too uncomfortable to ask. They know better but often skip this step because of how it makes them feel. They're so consumed with how they feel when they must ask for the sale that they don't think about how the prospect feels.

In the words of my dad, *if you don't ask, you won't get.* Prospective clients can't agree to work with you if you never ask the question. Not asking for the sale, especially if someone is a good prospect, is awkward. Think about how uncomfortable your client feels when you take up all of his time, discuss what you can do for him, share information about your services, and then don't bother to ask him for the business. While you're busy thinking about yourself and how uneasy you are, you never give a thought to how nervous your client feels.

The client is expecting you (if it's the right fit) to ask for the sale. Asking for the business is the natural progression in the sales process. It is the next part of the process, just as putting the cake in the oven is the next logical step in baking a cake that you can eat. Not making an attempt to close, or asking for the business, may cause the client to doubt you or your services. You send a silent message that indicates that you might not be the best choice.

If clients read apprehension in your body language, you won't close the sale. If you don't get comfortable asking for the business, you better get comfortable with prospects going to your competition.

If you don't ask, the answer is always no. It is your job to ask for the business! Prospects don't always let you know what's on their mind. *Sounds good, let's get started. I'm sold, I want to retain you right now.*

Some attorneys are afraid of being perceived as the stereotypical salesperson so commonly seen as brash, insistent, and obnoxious. They do anything they can to not be portrayed in that light. Even though the person they are speaking with is their ideal client, they zip their lips and don't ask for the business.

Because of a subconscious fear of being perceived as that cliché salesperson, all too often attorneys don't attempt to close the business. Or, if they do try to close the sale, they do not execute in a strong and assertive manner. Such attorneys may come across as wishy-washy or weak. You must ask for the business, or you won't have a business. You may do everything else right, but if you don't close correctly, there's no sale.

It may help a bit to think of it this way. Most people need you to help them in the decision-making process. You are the one to move them to a decision. Whether is it a yes or a no or a next month, prospects need you to nudge them in a way that causes them to take action in one direction or another.

Don't think of closing as pushing the prospect into doing something that he doesn't want to do. Instead, think of it as prompting him just enough to move him out of his inertia and into taking some kind of action.

If the fit is there and you can see yourself as the right attorney for this client, then not closing is a disservice to her. You might as well stop the meeting and drive a prospect to your competitor's office. You are preventing the prospect from deriving the benefits of your product or service.

If you think that selling or closing is unethical or distasteful, you must let that go. Delete from your mind the stereotypical perceptions of a closer and what it means to close the sale. Let go of thinking that you need to be hostile, forceful, or objectionable. If you feel that you must be over-zealous or offensive, your approach needs a shift. Good closing skills have nothing to do with hard-hitting rhetoric or well-rehearsed one-liners.

Many closing strategies have been around for decades. These strategies either no longer work like they used to or may rub prospects the wrong way. Wise prospective clients have heard them all.

Closing is easy and effortless when you have one or two unique closes of your own. Find language that you are most comfortable with that reflects your personality and style so that you may win the business.

Stalling, resisting, fearing, and attempting to shy away from this step will guarantee another lost sale.

You must complete the closing step. It is no different than running a marathon and stopping a few yards shy of the finish line. You are not done.

All you are doing when you ask for the sale is giving your client a gentle prod in the direction of a yes or a no. You never have to put him in a headlock, paint him into a corner, or tackle him to the ground to make a decision. You are simply asking him another question.

Last year, I received a call from Jeremy, the managing partner of a family law firm in Atlanta. He wanted to talk to me about doing an in-house training for the six attorneys in his firm. An attorney in his office had read my article about how the opening is the new closing. The article featured the top mistakes that attorneys make in the opening (the first three minutes) of a client consultation that cause them to not be able to close the business.

Jeremy asked if I could teach his attorneys how to be better closers and show them some more modern closing techniques. Jeremy informed me that over the past ninety days, his six attorneys had had approximately fifty-nine free initial consultations and only closed fifteen of them. We did some math together and estimated that more than $140,000 was lost to the competition.

Jeremy was convinced that the one skill missing in his attorneys' consultation process was how to close. Jeremy thought that they were losing clients and deals because they were bad closers.

I had to break the news to Jeremy that he was attempting to fix the wrong end of the problem and that teaching his attorneys how to close would not fix the issue. The attorneys were not losing business because they lacked a magical closing phrase or a slick closing technique that would compel a prospect to retain them on the spot.

They lacked the skills related to how to conduct a compelling client consultation from the beginning to the end, from the opening to the closing. They did not have the skills that would move an interested prospect into an invested client. The attorneys had not updated their process or shifted their approach or language in more than a decade. They were attempting to close today's consumer with an outdated sales process and old-school communication skills.

I explained that an attorney can't do an average or run-of-the-mill consultation and think that a new closing technique is going to win a client over. The best and most potent way to close more business is to recognize that closing starts at the beginning. Closing starts the moment that an attorney enters the consultation room, the moment that the conversation starts. The most important skill isn't closing, it's opening. The opening is the new closing.

Making superficial adjustments to the close will do nothing to increase profits. Fixing closing issues is like putting a Band-aid on a bullet would. If attorneys learn to open the right way, the prospective client will likely close himself. He will ask you how to get started and what next step he should take.

If the result of all of the hard work of attracting a prospect and meeting with her doesn't result in getting a new client or more business, it means that something is broken, something is off, something is in the way that is causing a prospect not to feel comfortable retaining you. She can't see the value that you provide. If you are not closing the business, it's a blatant indication of a larger and more costly problem.

The close is the easiest part of the process. Clients are rarely lost because you can't close. No one will ever tell you, *Marcus, you were my first choice, you're a superb attorney, and I would like to retain your services. Unfortunately, I can't. You're a crappy closer. Marie, I was hoping that you were going to be a more charismatic closer. I'm sorry, I won't work with an attorney who can't seal the deal with zest.*

No! The close is a result of a well-managed and thorough execution of the entire initial client consultation process. It's a natural culmination of a superlative conversation.

The reason why fixing closing problems is unproductive is that the result is only superficial. What's left untouched, what is missed, what is overlooked are the underlying dynamics that perpetuate the problem. If you want more clients, better results, and improved profits, you must be willing to fix the entire process. If it is fixed once, the dividends can be seen over and over.

The only way to stop the bleeding is to create a process that may be used in your consultations from start to finish. The process is in play from how you meet and greet the client to how you connect and communicate, from how and when to talk about yourself and your firm to how to handle objections with ease, from how and when to ask for the business to following up.

I'm not talking about some complicated, elaborate, or heavy-duty change. There is no long list of bullet points that you must remember or clever acronyms that you must memorize. You won't have to use complex scripts or uncomfortable closing techniques that don't feel good to you or your prospective client.

I'm talking about composing a natural approach that fits you like a custom-made coat. Once you put it on you will never take it off. I'm taking about making compelling shifts in your mindset and potent modifications in your skillset.

You invest a great deal of time, energy, and money to gain the attention of a prospective client, and he schedules time with you. To make the most of that consultation, from the opening to the closing, it's critical to understand what today's consumers need, want, and expect.

If you are unable to comfortably sell yourself and your services in initial client consultations, you will continue to leave enormous amounts of money on the table. You will continue to watch perfect clients walk out the door. You will continue to see money vanish before your eyes instead of profits pouring into your practice.

You have a short amount of time to win a prospect over and an even shorter amount of time to connect and make an impression. You have a limited amount of time to sell your expertise, build trust and credibility, to be different than the competition.

Many variables go into and lead to a victorious outcome in your initial consultations. Think of how many skills you use throughout your initial meeting alone that may make or break that meeting. These skills include how you introduce yourself, how to engage someone with thoughtful questions, how to gain trust from a total stranger, how to highlight your expertise and showcase your value, and how to discuss your fees and ask for the business.

Running parallel with these skills are the variables of your mental game: how are you coming across, are you exuding confidence, are your words making a connection, do you appear authentic and sincere, can you quiet your mind so that you may tune into your prospect, are you able to regulate your emotions when objections arise, do you present yourself with optimism and authority? All of this goes into an initial consultation, and it all contributes to the success or failure of that meeting.

Ask yourself if you are uncertain how to structure the consultation so that the client is able to recognize the value that you provide while educating her about your services. Are you clear about how to transition from talking about the prospect's legal issue to the services that you provide to asking for the business in a way that flows and feels natural? If not, do not have another consultation until you address this expensive issue.

One of the obstacles that I see in so many practices is the working harder versus working smarter concept. If sales are off and the numbers are down, attorneys believe that if they work harder, then sales will improve. This is not true.

Rather than accepting the fact that the game has changed and acquiring the skills to play in the new game, many attorneys believe that working harder is the answer. This is a form of denial. Attorneys block their transformation by denying that a problem exists. They are simply not willing to address the issue and admit that new ways of improving the game have come into vogue.

Collectively, lost revenue, clients leaving without retaining you, and profits dipping down are the equivalent of the check engine light going on in your car. This is a warning that you need to take action sooner rather than later. It is the difference between a $35 oil change and a $3,000 new transmission. Is a warning light going off in your practice? If so, don't wait until you need a complete overhaul. Get the good tune-up instead.

Knowing a few principles or techniques is not enough. You need to know them cold. My clients role-play this with me from opening to closing, discussing money and overcoming objections. They bake this conversation into their DNA. They own it. They use it to convert interested prospects into invested clients.

Closing is the logical conclusion to an effective and efficient process. Closing is the natural occurrence when you have completed all of the steps of the sales process.

Many attorneys remark, *I don't want to force someone to work with me. I don't want to pressure someone.* What? Who said anything about forcing someone to hire you? If you have to use force or pressure, your approach is all wrong. Get help.

Attorneys indicate that they don't want anyone to think that they are selling something. Really? You're not fooling anyone pretending that you are not selling something. You are, and everyone knows it. It's time to drop the disguise and be the noteworthy attorney behind your noteworthy services and expertise. You are selling yourself and your services.

You have an obligation to ask your client for some commitment. This looks different for each client, and you must keep the momentum going.

There are countless ways to ask for the business. Getting to this point and stopping the momentum is going to have to be a thing of the past. It is not your client's job to indicate to you that he is ready to get started or is ready to work with you. It's your job to make something happen next. All you have to do is ask.

Below are a few examples of ways to ask for the business. This list should be a good starting point for you. If the meeting is going well, pull out your audacity and ask:

- What are your thoughts about proceeding in this matter?
- When would you like to move forward and begin the process?
- Based on what we talked about, would you like me to prepare a retainer agreement or a proposal?
- Based on what you shared with me, it seems like a good fit. What do you think about retaining me to represent you?
- Now that you know more about my firm, are you comfortable moving forward?

Asking for the business using a fresh and modern approach like the above is more profitable for you and feels better for the client. It is up to you to discover ways to ask that best fit your style. When you discover one or two ways to ask for the sale, use them, own them, and allow them to leave your lips with aplomb.

Using outdated, stale, and predictable lines like those found below do nothing to differentiate you. If it was still 1972, these questions would work. But since it is not, strike them from the record:

- I think that we should sign the paperwork.
- Is there anything that you can think of that would keep us from working together?

- If fees were not a concern, would you do business with my firm?
- If you feel that you have everything you need to make a decision today, should we move forward?

The answer to these closing statements and questions usually results in prospects stating, *Let me think about it. I will call you next week.* Prospects may feel confronted with this kind of language and may feel forced into making an immediate decision.

It's your job to close and to find a way to do it that feels right for you. All parties involved should know what is going to happen next. Moving forward with complete clarity on both sides, making sure that everyone is on the same page, is an efficient way to do business.

I see too many attorneys get to this point in the process, and they ask for the business, but they use feeble closes. Many close by using language such as: *Well, let me know when you want to get started. Give me a call when you're ready. Keep me posted as to when the time is right for you.*

This may sound like a close, but it is not. It is up to you to ask for the sale. By simply changing the way that you ask for the business, you will automatically increase your closing percentage.

That's it! It's that simple. Taking the initiative to close the business shows confidence, strength, and clout. It shows that you believe in you and the services that you offer.

Chapter 17
Follow Up And Follow Through

Following up and following through are a critical part of the process but sadly have become the most neglected. There are many reasons why clients and business are lost, but one of the major reasons is poor or no follow up. Neglecting to finish what you've started shows a lack of attention on your part to your prospective clients. Why begin something if you have no intention of finishing it?

Attorneys who are serious about their practice follow up and follow through. When it comes to follow up, do you do what you say you're going to do when you say that you will do it? Or do you speak the words but lack the discipline to follow through? Not following up is an epidemic today, and this form of self-sabotage is completely within your control. I can't think of one good excuse for not following through.

Of course, sometimes things happen, or in a rare instance you do forget, but I am not talking about an occasional incident, I'm talking about blatant business negligence.

Think of a time when you started a discussion with someone that you considered doing business with. You took phone calls, participated in meetings, or exchanged e-mails and then got to the place where you were ready to give him your business. And then he disappeared. He dropped the ball. He left you surprised at his behavior and disappointed that he wasted your precious time.

In *Awaken The Giant Within*, Tony Robbins writes, *Everything you and I do, we do either out of our need to avoid pain or our desire to gain pleasure.*

In other words, people don't follow through because they associate more pain with doing the task than pleasure from completing it.

Tony states that the evidence does not lie.

> *If we link massive pain to any behavior or emotional pattern, we will avoid indulging in it at all costs. We can use this understanding to harness the force of pain and pleasure to change virtually anything in our lives.*

What is your poison, pain or pleasure?

A good follow up system will keep sales moving and keep your business in business. Clients respect efficient, organized, and dedicated business owners and professionals who follow through. When you follow up, you win clients.

Since few professionals follow up properly with clients, you will stand out when you do. Competent attorneys write things down, have a system in place to handle daily to-do tasks, return calls, keep their promises, and do what they say they will do.

In the business world some people think about it and talk about it, and some people do it. I challenge all attorneys, for twenty-one days, to stop talking about what they need to do and simply do it. If you tell a prospect that you will call her back, call her back. If you RSVP for an event, go to the event, don't pull a no-show. If you indicate that you will e-mail someone, send the e-mail. If you tell someone that you will take care of something, take care of it. Honor your word. Follow up and follow through. It will feel so good when you do. Give yourself an instant raise and follow up!

If you let your prospective clients fall through the cracks due to a lack of organization, failure to follow through, or poor communication, you may jeopardize your business, your professional reputation, and the potential for referrals. Poor communication or lack of responsiveness is a leading reason why clients leave businesses for a competitor. Being diligent in following up is a fine way to generate more sales.

Think about how much you have put into developing strategies, networking, and advertising. Dropping the ball at the follow up stage is counterproductive. It is not only unprofessional, it is bad business.

Chapter 18
Erasing The Time Excuse

I don't have enough time. That excuse is more common than the common cold. When life and work get busy, or when you don't want to feel guilty about avoiding a task or an obligation, the *I don't have enough time* excuse rolls off of your lips. Time, or lack thereof, is a lousy excuse for not becoming a rainmaker. Stop convincing yourself that you don't have the time to participate in client and business development activities.

The top rainmakers with whom I work have deleted the I-don't-have-enough-time money-robbing mantra from their vocabulary. You cannot manage time. You can only manage your priorities.

Jim Rohn says, *When you want to do something, you make the time. When you don't, you find an excuse.* How true. How many times a day or a week do you utter this income-killing phrase? Stop claiming that you don't have time and start taking ownership of the time that you do have.

Attorneys who have the right rainmaking attitude think, *Even though I'm busy, I will make time for marketing this week. I will work a few extra hours and network on LinkedIn. I will attend a bar association lunch meeting, even though my schedule is tight.* We all have the same twenty-four hours in a day. You are either using your time prudently or frittering it away.

Chronic excuse-making is an excellent way to evade doing the work. The only cure for this chronic condition is action. Astute attorneys know that if debilitating excuse-making is not cured, their practice may be trampled.

The bottom line is that we make up excuses to justify why we're not doing what we know we should do. It is time to enter the no-excuse zone! Stop making excuses for not using your time wisely and start making rain.

There is a stark difference between having time and prioritizing how you use the time that you have. Sure, things happen, and at times you may get busy and get pulled off of your business development plan, but making business development a priority is important to your success.

I am not going to go off on a time-management tirade because I don't believe that it is a time-management problem. It is a priority dilemma.

Face it. No one has enough time in the day for everything that they want to do. However, if something is a priority, you must make the time. Whenever you find yourself thinking, *I don't have time*, it may mean that that particular task is not a priority, or you didn't want to do it in the first place, so you blamed it on your lack of time. My belief is that *I haven't got the time* is code for *I haven't got the desire*.

Since no one has figured out how to add more hours to the day, the best that you can do is use the time that you do have more efficiently.

No miracle tool exists that will eliminate the work that we all have to do on a daily basis. However, some outstanding digital resources are available that may help you boost your efficiency. Below I have listed for you three free options. Don't like these? There are a dozen more to choose from.

RescueTime – This tool will hit you in the face with the stark reality of how much time you spend on websites like Facebook, Instagram, or Pinterest. This program runs in the background of your computer and mobile devices. RescueTime tracks how you spend your screen time and sends alerts when you've hit set time limits on specific websites or activities. The detailed analytics will help you understand where your time is going so that you may more easily eliminate whatever it is.

Boomerang for Gmail - If you spend late nights drafting e-mails and wait to send them until the next day so that they don't get lost in the overnight junk mail shuffle, install Boomerang instead. This Gmail app lets you schedule e-mails to be sent later, so you don't have to remember to re-visit your drafts in the morning. This free tool also sends reminders to you to follow up with someone if they haven't responded to your e-mail.

Unroll.me - Ever wonder how you ended up on some random e-mail list? Unsubscribing from these spam e-mails is super easy. Clean out your inbox with Unroll.me. You may unsubscribe from many e-mail lists with one click.

You may find many more time-saving apps, devices, and downloads to help you. Search for one or more of them that fits you and your lifestyle.

If you want something badly enough, and I mean you want it with your whole heart and soul, nothing will stop you, nothing will get in your way. Even mountains will crumble into molehills.

Hundreds of books and thousands of articles dispensing advice about how to manage your time are out there, but time-management skills are of no value if you don't know what things to manage or if you don't know what is a priority, what is important or urgent. Time is precious, it is not your enemy. It is important to figure out what is highest on the priority list and what can wait. Ask yourself, *is this urgent, important, or non-essential.*

Here come the excuses! Any of these sound familiar?

I'd like to get out of my office and network more, but I don't have time right now.

It would be great to grab a coffee and re-connect, but I don't know where I would find the time.

I should go to more conferences, but with my schedule, there's no time.

I know that I should be using LinkedIn. I've got to free up some time. I'll get to it tomorrow.

I know that I should go to the gym, but I am super busy and can't find the time.

I've worked myself to the bone, and I'm too tired to make the time.

The list goes on, but the theme is the same. People blame time itself for all of their incompletions, inefficiencies, lack of production, absence of income and clients. Blaming time is an easy and societally-acceptable excuse. But blaming time is nonsensical. Time is an inanimate object that has no vested interest in what you do with it. You cannot control much in life, but you can control the way that you spend your time.

Why would you want to broadcast to the world that your time-management skills are non-existent? Why would you announce to friends and co-workers that you don't know how to manage your life? Or worse, why would you demonstrate to clients that your lack of time-management abilities will cost them more in extra fees and billable hours?

The bottom line, the plain truth, the in-your-face reality is that blaming a lack of time for your failure to act usually means that you didn't want to complete the task in the first place. As a result, attorneys expend their valuable time and energy justifying their lack of performance instead of focusing on ways to improve it. They are becoming adept at the *I-don't-have-time* excuse.

I know how hard it can be. I am sympathetic to family and work commitments. But time is malleable, it may be stretched, it accommodates the committed, those searching for the holy grail of achievement.

We are all busy. Life is busy. You and I each have the same amount of time every day. Everyone on earth has one hundred and sixty-eight hours to divvy up throughout the week. It is what you do with your time that determines where your practice ends up. Pay attention to how many times a day you blame a lack of time for not getting things done.

It's not a matter of finding time, it's about making time for business activities. You must make your business a priority. This is no different than building time to exercise into your schedule. People who exercise regularly schedule exercise into their day as opposed to making excuses for not exercising. If getting things done is important to you, you must make the time. If you wait around to find the time, it will never happen.

Many attorneys have shared with me the frustration of the cycle that plays out over and over in their practice. Their business development efforts produce leads, which then garners a bit of business. Then they devote their time to client work. While they are focused on client work, they dial down their momentum in relation to networking, marketing, and sales, only to find themselves finishing up with one client with no prospects or new clients on the horizon.

The feast or famine cycle begins. Another wild ride on the revenue roller coaster. They have the dismaying task of starting the process of making rain all over again.

I often hear, *I'm too busy to do any marketing right now. I can't take the time for networking or sales. I need to focus on billing. The time that I spend selling is not billable time.* This distasteful ritual may be averted.

Many professionals with whom I work come up with the same excuses regarding their lack of time. It does not matter the profession, you still need to keep up the pursuit and make time to keep your client pipeline full. Time is not your adversary.

Recently I worked with Anne, an estate planning attorney, who was late for most of our coaching calls and ten to fifteen minutes late for her in-person client meetings. She always scrambled around at the last minute putting the final touches on her work.

Anne also racked up, in one year, $1,787 worth of speeding and parking tickets. Her insurance rates must have been sky high. But apparently they were not high enough and she was not suffering enough to change her ways. She was stuck in a vicious cycle.

As soon as our coaching sessions began and Anne finally got centered and ready, she made excuses. It took less than ten seconds for Anne to speed into her mantra. *I'm overwhelmed. I am super busy. I can hardly see straight. I worked until midnight last night. My weekends are filled with work.*

Her default rants were on auto-pilot. Doom and gloom were her specialty. And *poor me* was always the theme of her day. She got up every day and pinned on her busy badge.

One day, in particular, I tried something different with Anne. As her coach, it was my obligation to tackle this issue that was getting in the way of our sessions and her greatness. A gigantic obstacle sat squarely in the way of a breakthrough. Time!

She was inflamed, as usual. "All I do is work. My clients want everything for nothing, and I'm not making any money. My clients are sucking the life out of me."

I remained calm. "Please take a breath, and pause for a second. Have you ever noticed that you blame time for everything? It appears that you are making time your enemy. It seems that you may like flying by the seat of your pants. It sounds like you think that being so busy that you can't see straight is admirable? Are you open to trying something different for thirty days?"

"Uh...well...maybe. What do you have in mind? Well... actually...I'm not sure. I might be too busy...to try something new. I might not have time." Anne floundered.

"For the next month, I advocate that you stop declaring to everyone you meet how super busy you are. Which by the way, no one cares, they are busy too. It is no longer a symbol of honor to wear your busy badge. Take off your busy badge, and look at how you spend your time.

"What if when you find yourself blaming time, you turn your finger around and point it back at yourself. What could you learn? How could you stop time from running away from you? What could you do right now to be productive?"

She got quiet and was not sure what to do with that. She expected me to do what everyone else did when she went off on her rant. She expected me to listen, offer my condolences, and accept her invitation to the pity party. Wrong!

She paused and then spoke in a tiny voice. "Hmmm, I guess if I don't figure out why time keeps getting away from me, I will never be the rainmaker that I have vowed to be. I have been this way for most of my career. Can you help? Can you hold my feet to the fire and help me have a breakthrough?"

"Of course. That's what I'm here for."

Anne needed a plan, someone to hold her to a higher standard and help her become accountable to herself. That's when things slowly began to change.

Anne now asks herself, "What may I do to rise above my circumstances and achieve the results for which I strive?"

Being responsible for how you use your time is the process of seeing it, owning it, solving it, controlling it, and doing it. Scrutinizing your use of time requires a level of ownership that includes doing what is necessary and focusing on proactive accountability, not reactive excuses.

Excuses keep you stuck in the same holding pattern of not being responsible. Excuse-making is not the conduit to rainmaking, surrendering your busy badge is.

Anne has informed me that she no longer collects parking and speeding tickets. She has slowed down and is now deliberate in how she chooses to spend her time.

Do you have a busy badge that needs to be relinquished?

Chapter 19
The Trust Factor: Get It And Keep It

So much has changed in the world of business, but some things have not. Building trust was important five or six decades ago, and it's just as important today.

If building relationships is the key to success, then trust is the foundation. Unfortunately, today's consumers are busier than ever and have access to more information and choices. They're looking for an attorney whom they know that they can trust to work in their best interests.

The building of a relationship with a client is not a separate activity that takes place before or after a meeting. It is inherent in every meeting or consultation.

Most new client interactions begin with high tension and low levels of trust. Moving your prospective client from a low-trust, high-tension level to a high-trust, low-tension state is essential. When you reach a level of high trust and low tension, your prospect stops resisting and begin to see you as her only choice.

We all buy from people whom we trust. That's why it's so important to take the time to build rapport throughout your process. Make it a priority. Selling is about relating, not persuading.

Trust does not depend on the length of time that two people have known each other. Trust depends on the depth of understanding that develops between them. Your reputation for being trustworthy is something that you strengthen over time with a steady, positive performance.

However, your prospects are coming to the table with a little less trust than in the past. The bar on trust is set low, and you may have to actively work to raise that level of trust.

We size people up based on the way that they communicate with us, and we do this swiftly. It all comes down to whether someone trusts you. There is a fine line but a clear distinction between rapport and trust, but this is often missed by inexperienced attorneys.

Before you pick up the phone to call a prospect or conduct an initial meeting, make sure that you plan to earn trust by design, not default. Make sure that you will be able to see things from the other person's point of view. Your prospects should leave a meeting with you thinking, *She is a fantastic listener. He can help us with our business issue. She made me feel comfortable and put me at ease. I can see myself working with him.*

Think of a time when you met someone for the first time and the conversation felt natural, comfortable, and tension-free. You could see that you were a good fit.

Do your prospective clients trust what you say? Do they trust you as an attorney? Skilled attorneys gather information in a natural manner that gets clients to open up. Talented attorneys shine the spotlight on and focus their attention on their clients.

Prospects may come to your meeting painting all attorneys with the same brush. To them, all attorneys are made from the same mold and should not be trusted. Make sure that you take the paintbrush out of the client's hand by acting in a manner that engenders instant trust.

Building trust does not happen overnight. It's the many little things that you do over time that helps you build lasting relationships. It is honoring your word; following through; timely visits, calls, and response to e-mails; and problem solving, to name a few, that all add up to trust.

Developing trust is essential. Without it, you don't have a prayer of getting the business. With it, you'll have an opportunity to grow your book of business and a profitable practice. It is worth the extra effort.

Chapter 20
Don't Overcome Objections, Handle Them Instead

Why do you hear objections? What do they mean? From here on out, learn to treat objections as if a prospect is saying, *I am not sold on the details that you've presented so far. Could you please give me more information so that I might make an educated decision?* Your prospect needs more from you so that she may confidently say yes.

Objections that you'll come across include: *Your fees are too expensive. This won't work for me. This all sounds too complicated. This is going to be too hard to accomplish. Now is not the right time.*

When you get an objection, all you have to do is acknowledge it, diffuse it, and address a prospect's concerns around the objection. Don't utter a snappy comeback. Understand what the client is saying. When you do, your conversations will remain comfortable and authentic, which is what prospects always want in the end.

When a potential client gives you any kind of objection, most of the time they're telling you that they're interested, but there is something standing in the way of saying yes. Objections may arise from a client who wants his doubts clarified, or he needs further information or reassurance about certain points. People don't ask questions and have objections unless they are seriously considering you and your service.

View the objection as a request for more information or as a prospect's concern or fear. Every objection provides you with a new opportunity to share the right information with a prospect and to move them into the next step of your sales process.

When a client voices a concern, never interrupt her and jump in and overcome the objection. The more she talks, the more comfortable she will feel with you, and the more you will learn about concerns that she has. Make it a point to never disagree, because that will alienate the client by proving that you think she is wrong. You may win the war of words, but you will lose the sale.

Let's face it. Buying can be a scary step. People will have legitimate concerns. It is an important part of your job to help prospects work through these fears and concerns. Your job isn't to overcome objections. Your job is to help your client be strong, be clear, and stay focused so that she can do what's right for her.

How you view and handle objections may have a significant impact on the outcome of the conversation. You can't work around objections, ignore them, or pretend that they are not there. There is a barrier between you and your prospect, and together you need to take it down. Be mindful of this. Recognize your tendency to feel defensive, and replace this with empathy and curiosity.

If you pressure someone, they'll stop trusting you. A loss of trust always means the loss of the sale. But if someone makes himself vulnerable by expressing objections and you listen and don't attack, he relaxes, remains open, and feels safe. And you may move forward without a hitch or hindrance.

If you keep yourself centered and calm instead of becoming fearful or confrontational, you then may diffuse the objection and re-open the sales conversation. This in turn allows you to help your prospective client be truthful about his situation so that he doesn't feel threatened. He needs to feel sure that if he makes himself vulnerable with you, you won't take advantage of the information that he shares and try to hard-sell him your solution.

Objection! Just the word makes some people shudder. Why? Because it could mean that rejection is coming. Or it could mean that opportunity is on the way.

Your reaction to objections has a giant impact on your ability to work through the objection to the satisfaction of your client.

During your initial consultations, it is common that some sort of objection will come up. Think of it as a concern or a question about the fit of the solution or the next step.

When an objection is stated, both parties have a stake in the outcome. How you handle the objection, not overcome it, may make or break what happens next. Most people have a fight-or-flight response to an objection.

Client Objection: *We would really like to move forward and start working with you, but your fees are much higher than two other attorneys that we are considering.*

The typical old-school response: *Well, they are both good attorneys, but neither one of them specializes in X and Y. They are not experts in your exact situation. My fees are worth it because I will provide you with excellent this and momentous that... Blah, blah, blah.*

All of this sounds to the prospective client like a mammoth justification, not a compelling reason why your fees are higher. It is your job to get underneath the objection and gain a better understanding of her objection.

My suggested response: *I appreciate you telling me that I am your top choice and that you would like to retain me. However, it sounds like my higher fees are a stumbling block and that you would like to discuss them a bit more? Is that correct?*

Let's take a step back and re-visit some of the specialized services that you are looking for and how I deliver them. Then we can talk about how those fees specifically work into the overall plan. How does that sound?

Next time you hear an objection, don't panic and think that you have to fight back and go into justification mode. Go into

problem-solver mode instead. Below are three steps that you may use to handle any objection.
1. Acknowledge the objection.
2. Probe for clarity.
3. Answer with relevant information.

As you enter into any sales dialogue, you may encounter objections. Don't fear them. Don't allow them to derail the conversation. Meet them head-on using your new three-step plan.

Chapter 21
Networking Essentials

Networking is a productive way to build professional relationships and find new business opportunities. Networking is a reciprocal process based on the exchange of ideas, advice, and referrals. Having a networking strategy is invaluable.

The most formidable aspect of networking is also the hardest. You have to put yourself out there. You have to be out in the marketplace and expose yourself to people who do not know you.

As you embark on networking activities, it is critical that you change your mindset to a positive one. If you see networking as an unpleasant and time-wasting task, your efforts will not be rewarding. Find a way to get comfortable with networking because it will make all the difference in your revenue stream.

You can network anywhere. Relationships are started and cultivated by anything from attending an after-hours business event to going to a football game. You may begin a relationship at the theater, the health club, a child's birthday party, or a concert. You just need to be where other people like you, or people that you want to meet, congregate.

Not all connections are beneficial, nor do they lead to clients or business. They're just connections, and that is fine.

Bright people begin a connection with casual conversation, thought-provoking questions, and meaningful dialogue so that they may get to know the other person.

The object of making a connection is to make a good one, one that is friendly and solid. When you connect in a positive way, you create a reputation at the same time.

Be interesting and memorable. This seems simple, right? You can't feature how many people go to events and converse about the same monotonous things and ask the same lame questions to everyone they meet. Use your imagination.

For many, networking comes naturally. For others, it must be learned and continuously honed. Not everyone is excited about attending networking events. Like it or not, you have to do it. Yes, it may be uncomfortable walking into a room full of strangers or attending a conference or trade show where you do not know anyone, but this is not an excuse for skipping this practice-building activity.

Networking is one of those activities that may easily fall off of your calendar. Just like exercising, you may skip a workout or tell yourself that you are too busy to exercise. Networking doesn't just happen. It has to be part of your marketing plan. Networking must be incorporated into your schedule and written on your calendar.

I talk to many attorneys who insist that they tried networking, and it did not work for them. They told me that it was a waste of time and that they never met anyone who became a client. Their self-fulfilling prophecy took center stage.

They went to a networking event without the right mindset. Showing up at a networking event without having a plan almost guarantees that it will be a waste of time.

When you declare that something will turn out badly or not go your way, it will. Have you ever started your morning and knew that it was going to be a bad day? Sure enough, you stub your toe, your garage door won't open, traffic is terrible. A series of negative things just seem to happen. This is a self-fulfilling prophecy. A self-fulfilling prophecy is when someone unknowingly causes a prediction to come true, due to the simple fact that he expects it to come true. Pay attention to what you think before networking.

Some networkers go to an event armed with a stack of business cards to give to anyone with hands. Their sole intention is to pass out cards and then wait for someone to contact them afterwards. That is not how building relationships works. The best strategy is to make it your intention to collect business cards, not distribute them.

Gathering business cards puts the follow up initiative in your court instead of relying on someone else to contact you. You take the lead. You initiate the next move. You start the relationship. This is no different than building friendships for purposes of finding a mate. The goal of networking is to make contacts and get information that leads to relationships. It takes two to tango. Start dancing, and network in a proactive way, not a passive way.

Being proactive puts you in the driver's seat. You are in complete control of what does and does not happen when you network.

Some of the wise rainmakers that I have worked have allowed me to share with you below the networking mantras that work for them:

- I will build my network and relationships with consistency, intensity, and enthusiasm. I will no longer be haphazard in my approach. Irregular and unproductive networking does not work.
- My network is my top priority, and I will devote significant effort to building my network. I will use the plan and strategy that I have in place.
- Cultivating new relationships is not something to add to my to-do list. I will put it on my must-get-done list.
- Expanding my network is no longer on the back-burner for me. I will actively pursue new business and nurture relationships as they grow and strengthen.
- I will meet and interact with people during my business activities. I will work proactively to build my network and relationships.
- I will follow up when I return from every event. No more allowing a stack of business cards and new contacts to go to waste.

Many attorneys fail to yield any revenue from networking not only because of what they do at the event but because of what they fail to do afterward. Why? They are horrible at following up. They do not follow through. Networking is a waste of time if you don't follow up. Enormous amounts of time, money, and energy are spent attending conferences, trade shows, and professional organization meetings with little to show for it in the end.

Let's imagine that you or your firm is participating in a trade show. You may have invested thousands of dollars on exhibits, promotional items, and travel expenses but invested little time and money in devising a solid follow up strategy to make later contact with people that you meet.

For example, perhaps a dozen prospects come to your booth, and you visit with these folks. Many of them tell you that they are interested in having a longer conversation after the trade show. You agree to keep the ball in play and follow up with the prospect after the show. You honor your agreement and call your new connection.

I will assume that you are leaving a voicemail, using typical, generic, and lackluster language, such as, *Hi, Alice, it was nice to meet you at the ABC conference. Hope you had a great time. It has been a week, and I wanted to follow up with you and finish our conversation. I may be reached at XXX-XXX-XXXX. I look forward to hearing from you.*

Guess what? Everyone else who met your new connection at the trade show is leaving the same hollow message. Every voicemail sounds the same.

Nothing in your message made you stand out. Nothing in your message was unforgettable or would trigger a memory of who you are and what you do. Unfortunately, your message does not warrant a return call. It is deleted with all of the others.

After waiting for a couple of days, you send an e-mail, and you wind up communicating almost the same thing in your e-mail. Next, you call the prospect again, leaving another message that resembles the first message, only you add a few words. *I'm not sure if you got my last message, but I wanted to follow up with you...*

You do not include a strong call to action! You do not articulate anything that could be considered engaging. Just following up is not enough. You must leave a message and deliver something in your follow up that would compel someone to call you back. Otherwise, you blend in, you do not stand out.

Hypothetically, you promised to follow up with thirty people after the event. Your standard follow up strategy leads to no return calls, no responses to e-mails, and no new business. Without a robust and strategic follow up plan, these efforts fail miserably.

When I work with my clients, we devise pre-event, at-the-event, and post-event strategies to maximize effectiveness and profitability. Many attorneys swear that they have a plan, but that plan disintegrates when they return to their office and resume their lives. They get busy. Stuff gets in the way. Or the plan that is in their head is the generic type that I just described. This is obviously not going to be profitable.

These expensive and time-consuming networking events produce no results. The attorneys with whom I work tell me that they go to events and rarely get any business from them.

Not following up after an event does nothing to make you stand out and differentiate yourself. If you are going to invest the time and money into networking, why not invest as well in a strategic follow up system.

It is much more worthwhile to construct a plan that works for you. I am happy to assist you with devising a plan that fits your style.

Gaining business from networking comes down to being diligent in your follow up. Following up seems to be the most difficult skill to master and the most harrowing to undertake. That's unfortunate because a solid follow up plan makes networking fruitful instead of fruitless.

You must have conversations that are memorable, valuable, and personable so that the people you meet will take your call a week after an event.

Below are five things that clever networkers do:
- Prepare for the event by researching the attendees and developing interesting questions and talking points.
- Attempt to connect with attendees on social media or LinkedIn prior to the event so that you may see faces and others may see yours.
- Connect with new people at the event, and get their contact information. Follow up with them. I tell the people whom I meet that I would be happy to take the follow up off of their plate and communicate with them when I return to my office.
- Follow up swiftly and be politely persistent.
- Continue to stay connected and communicate through social media.

When attempting to increase the number of your business relationships, having a networking strategy will make your efforts more valuable and pleasurable.

Chapter 22
Business Networking Made Easy

Sharp networkers know how to work a room! Productive networkers know how to convert their connections into clients and close deals. Strong networkers are easy to spot. They circulate with grace and ease, meeting, greeting, and talking to people in a way that looks and sounds sincere. It's obvious that they know how to start, develop, and end lively and interesting conversations that enhance rapport.

Working a room means having many short conversations with many people. But short doesn't mean superficial.

It's possible to have meaningful and stimulating short conversations with new contacts that yield connections and make you memorable.

Many attorneys attend networking events with good intentions of meeting people and cultivating new relationships. Not everyone goes with the same good intentions. Some are only attending to hunt for prey and seem more interested in stalking others and finding new victims.

Networking isn't about hunting for prospects, it's about making contacts that eventually lead to a connection. The networker who works a room with a *what's in it for me* attitude will never find new clients.

Working a room is not about buzzing around and pressing your cards into the palms of anyone with a free hand. Networking is not about haphazardly having fleeting half-conversations with other people. Sure, you will meet a lot of people if you do this, but it is unlikely that you will make a splash. If you do, it won't be a favorable one.

When you know how to work a room, you feel better about yourself, you make many social and business contacts, and you make others feel more comfortable too. Your particular way of being will attract people to you and make them want to know you better.

Next time you are at an event, make a conscious decision to approach people to whom you might not normally speak. Armed with your repertoire of conversation-starters and questions, you should have no difficulty in making a good first impression and developing rapport. The more people you meet in a genuine way, the less fazed you will be by the networking process. It's all a part of the big networking plan of working a room to your advantage.

Below are a few conversation-starters to help you open up a dialogue and recommendations to keep the conversation going:

- What types of projects are you working on right now?
- Are you working on anything new or exciting?
- I'm curious about how you landed in your line of work?
- Are you staying in town for the holidays?
- What types of networking events do you enjoy going to?
- What do you like to do in your spare time?
- Have you been to an event like this before?
- How long have you been involved in this organization?
- Do you belong to any other organization that you recommend?

Have a few go-to questions that feel right for you in your mind ahead of time.

Another important tip to remember when you are working a room is not to be in sales mode. Move gently from a social to a business conversation, and avoid any appearance of selling. People aren't at networking events to buy or be sold, they're there to network.

You must network if you want to grow your business and get more referrals. You must be willing to have interesting conversations with many new people. I tell my clients that unless their phone is ringing off the hook and they have more business than they can handle, they must network on a regular basis.

Get out there, and work the room like a pro. It is one of the best ways to grow your practice.

Many attorneys believe that who you know is just as important as what you know. Having a rainmaking business depends as much on people skills as it does on qualifications and experience. You may find it more difficult to achieve the prosperity that you deserve if your skill set is unbalanced, loads of one and not much of the other.

No matter how brilliant you are or how much you know about the law, if you want to get ahead, good connections will help. Getting to know people and making new connections is an essential part of growing your practice and making rain.

One important thing to remember while networking is that it helps to be curious about other people. Others will find you far more interesting if you show an interest in them. Learn the fine art of networking. And remember that it is not about you.

Being generous and courteous to others makes you memorable and is a wonderful networking asset.

As you begin to network, the key will lie in your ability to be flexible.

Using the same approach over and over again in networking will not produce different results. And why should it? No one person is the same as another, so why should repeating the same introductory remarks and conversational opening statements be right for every contact and occasion? Be flexible and honest.

Be confident, and become adept at trying new approaches, and you will succeed. Once you get used to networking and make progress with relationship-building, the motivation to continue will be high.

Those who appreciate networking find it fun and exciting. For those who don't like networking, it may be intimidating and scary.

But it is the best way to overcome shyness, discover unexpected opportunities, increase sales, and develop new relationships.

You may be reluctant to take the first steps, whether from fear or lack of time, but a positive outlook is vital to relationship-building. Once you learn how to make connections in a way that feels comfortable for you, you'll put the bashfulness behind you and get excited about networking. Once you have broken down the barriers that up to this point have prevented you from trying, you'll feel different about networking.

Be interested in others rather than forcing others to be interested in you. When you are generous to those you meet, you will find the motivation to identify opportunities through your positive mental attitude.

Chapter 23
Modern Marketing Methods

Those in the traditional marketing arena have always maintained that to market properly, you must be willing to invest a fair amount of money. Modern marketing methods show that if you are willing to invest intangibles, such as intention and imagination, you will see results. Many of these modern marketing formulas, thanks to the Internet, are free or budget-friendly. Don't underestimate the vitality of these methods because they don't require a large financial investment on your part.

Traditional marketers believe that you can seal the deal with marketing alone. Modern marketers know that when your goal is to generate interest, to make people want to know more, and to build a brand, you're marketing. If your goal is to get a consumer to exchange money for your product or service, you're selling.

Marketing with technology has exploded, and there is no shortage of information about it and gurus to show you how. Buyer beware. This is where the problem starts. When it comes to marketing, the missing link is often execution. Information is never the problem these days, implementation is the problem.

Where do I start? How do I put the pieces together? How do I make sure that my marketing rockets hit the right target?

I will provide you with a starting point for your marketing efforts, though the options are endless. I will boil it down to a few straightforward tips, tools, and techniques so that you may move into action. My goal is to keep you from bobbing on an inner tube in the sea of competition, waiting to see where the current takes you.

Marketing consistency is more important than your marketing intensity. Winning and keeping clients is the result of an effective and steady marketing strategy. The paramount question that you will always be asking yourself is: *What specific actions do I want my prospective client to take as a result of my marketing efforts? Do I want her to schedule an appointment, download a brochure, call my office, or send me an e-mail?*

You can't be everything to everyone. In marketing, knowing where not to play is as important as knowing where to play. You may already know that you are not going to market yourself on local television, but you do know that you want to contribute articles to an industry trade magazine. Or perhaps you know that cold calling is not in the cards for you, but pursuing warm leads through a referral system is more in line with your personality and practice goals.

By now you should already know who your ideal clients are and have the ability to zero in on them for your marketing endeavors. Identifying legitimate clients will help ensure that your marketing arrow hits the bull's eye.

I will assume that your marketing goal is to increase visibility, credibility, and profitability. It is to attract more clients and close more business.

You may have superb selling skills. You may have mastered every step in the selling process: opening meetings, conducting the needs analysis, presenting recommendations, discussing fees, and closing the business. But if you aren't meeting with prospective clients and finding opportunities to execute the steps of the sales process, what good are those selling skills doing you? Get out and use your marketing skills to market yourself and attract and close more business.

Marketing skills are the key to sales success. You need both sets of skills. Your performance today is dependent upon your aptitude as a marketer as well as your ability as a salesperson. Your mindset as a marketer needs to change, and your sales skills need to keep pace.

Chapter 24
Social Media Marketing: Increasing Your Visibility And Credibility

The Internet is the greatest communication tool of all time. Buckle up. This is the way in which communication is going. It is coming at you in a 24/7, always-on environment. The goal of marketing has always been to compel people to notice you, trust you, and then take action. What's different now is that the tools are constantly changing.

Business as you know it is transforming itself right before your eyes. It is waiting for you to get on board and hang on for the ride of your life or get left in the proverbial dust. The moment has come to learn and adapt.

Do you want to be safe and predictable or bold and victorious?

The great game-changing aspect of social media marketing is that it exponentially reduces the time required to become a trusted advisor within your sphere of expertise. Visibility establishes credibility.

If you are seen as a qualified expert by those in the marketplace, if you are a source for timely, relevant information in which those whom you desire to influence may find benefit, then people in the marketplace will come to you to obtain your advice.

In other words, if you provide people with fresh and innovative ideas, they will hire you primarily because they value your opinion.

I am sure that you have heard that people like to buy from people with whom they are familiar. The reason is simple: in a world of choices, the more familiar you are to your prospective buyer, the less the perception of risk in doing business with you.

If you're like many attorneys, you have more than a little trepidation about entering the digital and social media marketplace. Social media and technology have leveled the playing field for everyone in every industry. They have changed the way that people connect, communicate, and do business. Technology and social media have transformed the world and brought forth change greater than at any other period in history. This change is so widespread that it is hard to imagine a time when we lived without the Internet and smartphones, tablets, and myriad other devices.

Building a booming practice has never been easier with the tools of technology available today. Technology enables attorneys to market their services and sell themselves without spending a fortune. If you have not yet embraced social media, run, don't walk, and join the more than three hundred million people using social media. You won't regret it.

You may come up with several excuses, a dozen reasons, and lots of justifications why you don't have time to market online. But none of these excuses, reasons, or justifications will hold water. A marketing attitude shift is in the making.

Along with a good marketing attitude, you need solid marketing habits. It's difficult to market on a steady basis unless you have a plan or a system in place. Your goal is to develop superior marketing habits that are so automatic that you don't have to think about them.

Whatever you decide about marketing your services, do it daily. Otherwise, your efforts will be difficult to track and measure. Treat your marketing efforts as seriously as you do your work with clients.

Social media and technology are not going away any time soon. Now everyone may tap into the exuberance of technology and grow their practice and build relationships. The best part of online marketing is that it is either low-cost or free.

You cannot afford to ignore the effect that online marketing and social media has had on the legal profession. What used to work no longer does. What got you to where you are today won't keep you there tomorrow. Attorneys who do not embrace online marketing will find themselves locked out of the world's best way to grow their practice.

Sole practitioners may use social media to market themselves online and compete against much larger firms. On social media, size does not matter. The size of your firm has little to do with your visibility and credibility. The opportunities are endless for attorneys who are willing to invest time and energy in growing their online presence.

Social media keeps you top-of-mind with others. You are more likely to find opportunities and business if you have a strong presence on social media. Intermittent or no presence on social media, particularly on LinkedIn, sends a negative message to your potential clients. It could be a sign that you are not that serious, that you are lazy, that you are not technologically on the ball, or that your thinking has not kept up with the times.

Social media is no longer optional. It is critical if you wish to have an affluent practice.

Free Or Low-Cost Ways To Use Social Media And Technology:
- Have a presence on Facebook, Twitter, and LinkedIn.
- Post a video or podcast from an article that you wrote.
- Write your own blog and/or contribute to other blogs.
- Write for online magazines, industry journals, or e-books.
- Host a webinar or a teleseminar about a hot industry topic or a newsworthy event.
- Send out an electronic newsletter.

The social media landscape is changing at lightening speed. Ideas available to you to grow your practice are endless.

No matter what strategies you choose, make sure that you enjoy them.

The top three social media sites for attorneys are LinkedIn, Facebook, and Twitter.

Plenty of books, articles, classes, and resources are available to help you decide which of these platforms you would like to try first. Spend some time researching the ones that will work best for you and your practice. Or please feel free to contact me, and I will brainstorm with you so that we may find a few ideas that will work in your practice.

Chapter 25
Locking In Business Using LinkedIn

LinkedIn is the social network of choice used by professionals for networking and making connections. LinkedIn allows you to network with people all over the world, not just across town. Understanding how to use LinkedIn to your advantage may help you expand your reach and multiply your connections in ways that you never imagined possible. LinkedIn is the ultimate business power tool that gives you the ability to build and control your personal online brand, increasing the chances of relevant decision-makers finding you online.

If Facebook is for your personal network, friends and family, LinkedIn is for your business network.

I used LinkedIn while researching this book. I connected with attorneys in the practice areas of divorce, personal injury, bankruptcy, and estate planning. I sent out forty-five personalized requests asking each attorney if he or she was open to answering a few questions in exchange for some free coaching.

I was blown away by the kindness and speediness with which they responded to my SOS. Thirty-three out of forty-five attorneys took me up on my offer. Each attorney provided me with priceless information.

Ten short years ago, marketing and selling were much different than they are today. The Internet hadn't yet developed into its current state, and the ability to connect with a massive audience of targeted prospects was available only to large corporations with huge marketing budgets.

Today, marketing, selling, and the Internet could not be more closely intertwined. These days, even a solo attorney on a tight budget may leverage online tools to reach a wide audience.

Anyone may use LinkedIn, but the site is most beneficial for attorneys looking to network online, grow their practices, and broaden professional connections.

The basic service is free. The site lets you search for and find business associates, clients, and colleagues whom you already know. You connect with them through the site, and they become part of your network.

LinkedIn also offers users the ability to have a paid account. You may be wondering if it is necessary to pay for LinkedIn. While there are a few additional benefits to upgrading your account, most people do not even fully utilize the standard, free version. For that reason, I would start with the free account and work up to the upgrades, should you need to access more information.

When you leverage the might that is LinkedIn, you will find possibilities today that never existed before. The only hurdle to get over is that these technologies are new. Implementing them means learning specialized techniques that you've never used before. But this actually works for you, because by reading this book and putting a plan into action, you will be getting a big jump on your competitors.

The trick to using LinkedIn is to not overthink it. Stop stressing out about having to add another new something-to-learn to your to-do list. LinkedIn is an online networking tool that isn't going anywhere. If you have not yet dipped your toe in, it's not too late. I would advise you to take the plunge and familiarize yourself with LinkedIn right now.

Once you start to harness the marketing potential of LinkedIn, you don't then need to abandon everything else. Face-to-face networking and in-person meetings still have tremendous value and will always play a part in your business development strategy. But you don't have to rely solely on those things anymore! You now get to prospect and market online and offline. It's not a case of doing one or the other, you'll do both.

I found an additional eight to ten extra hours per week by trading two face-to-face networking meetings with utilizing a LinkedIn strategy. I now network all over the world without ever leaving my office. What a great use of my time! Networking does not have to eat up all of your precious time.

A strong LinkedIn presence has become a must-have as opposed to a nice-to-have for all professionals. Using technology and mastering certain social media platforms isn't brain surgery. It is a skill that, once integrated into your practice, will help you increase your impact, influence, and income.

Follow these instructions on how to build a strong presence on LinkedIn:

- Create an account on LinkedIn at www.linkedin.com.
- Fill out your profile completely. Include your current place of employment and contact information (website, e-mail address, and phone number).
- Think of an attention-getting headline.
- Post a professional-looking picture of yourself.
- Include a background image.
- Expand your summary and your experience, if necessary.
- Add media or a video that supports your stated expertise.
- Upload your existing contacts from your e-mail account or other databases that you may have.
- Join seven to ten LinkedIn groups that cater to your industry/purpose/area of interest.
- Use this incredible tool to explode your profits.

And please feel free to use my profile as an example: https://www.linkedin.com/in/lizwendling.

You can always go back and refine or add to your profile later. For now, just do it. It will be worth the time investment.

Because I have seen so many attorneys resist learning how to use LinkedIn, I designed a LinkedIn Boot Camp that shortens their learning curve, teaches them how to use it in their practice, and pushes them out into the online world faster than they could do it themselves.

Technology is evolving at breakneck speed. LinkedIn is becoming the go-to communication tool for professionals. Like it or not, technology has triggered irreversible changes in the way that we do just about everything. Technology has forever changed the way that business gets done.

Business as usual has officially departed. The influence that social media has had in today's society is astounding. You must no longer sit on the sidelines. You have two options: you can resist and fade away, or you can adapt and flourish.

We are in such a virtually connected world that not having a LinkedIn profile, or even the right kind of profile, will work against you. The lack of a LinkedIn presence will make you invisible to your prospective clients. While people used to gauge the visibility and trustworthiness of an attorney or a firm through traditional means, such as how big a yellow pages ad was or word of mouth referrals, today they are doing it via technology. This is why it is so critical to develop a strong online presence.

The good news is that if you take a bit of time to learn how to use LinkedIn, this will help you grow your practice like nothing that has come before. The bad news? If you don't adapt to this fundamentally new way of doing business, you may find yourself missing opportunities.

For now, take a break, and get comfortable with the idea of using LinkedIn every day. A few minutes a day on LinkedIn, with time and commitment, will produce amazing results.

Developing and learning to manage your LinkedIn presence is one of the best tools available for taking control of your professional destiny. Your competitors are already there, it's time to join them.

The goal of the site is to allow registered members to develop networks of people whom they know and trust professionally. I recommend it to all of my clients. Why? Your current and prospective clients are already there. They are looking for you to be there too.

Once you've connected with someone, you will then have access to their list of connections. This is called your extended network. You may request an introduction to people in your extended network through your mutual contact.

When you meet a prospective client at an event or a business function and leave your business card with them, in all likelihood they will search for you on LinkedIn. Will you be found if they look?

You can't ignore this hard-core fact. Your potential clients will use the Internet and social media before they think about finding you another way.

People are busier than ever, and they are spending more and more time online. If they look at your LinkedIn profile and determine that you are credible and that you represent yourself and your firm well, that saves them time. Every clever attorney that I know uses LinkedIn to learn more about the people and the companies that he or she is thinking about doing business with.

Having a robust LinkedIn profile that portrays you as the ace attorney that you are is an important tool in strengthening your online credibility. If you're not using LinkedIn to its full capabilities, rest assured that you're leaving a lot of money on the table. I guarantee that your competitors are either already on the LinkedIn bandwagon or are scrambling to get there.

By not having a presence on LinkedIn, an attorney is telling the entire business community that he is not open for business. Failing to stay current will force you into professional obscurity.

If you are using LinkedIn or other social media, you must persistently ask yourself if your presence online supports your offline reputation as an attorney who is seen as an expert and as someone who may be trusted. Does your profile help your prospective clients view you as a credible resource with a trusted reputation? If you answered no, it's time for some minor adjustments or a full-blown profile makeover.

Prospects may look you up online in an effort to get a sense of who you are and what you are all about prior to meeting with you. What they find will cause them to make instant judgments about you. Those judgments will reflect your ability to influence and inspire them. Most people make split-second judgments about others. Those first impressions, regardless of how valid they are, are real and cannot be overlooked.

Your LinkedIn profile is a direct reflection of you and your practice. Until your prospect meets you by phone or in person, who you are online is who you are. Invest time in developing and perfecting your LinkedIn profile, making sure that your online image casts you in the best possible light.

I have heard that in the physical world, you sometimes get a second chance to make a good first impression. In the virtual world, you have zero chance of changing a negative first impression. When potential clients view the virtual version of you and don't like what they see, they find someone else.

Start by creating a professional, polished, and complete LinkedIn profile. This profile is used to network, engage, and connect with other professionals.

Unless you are looking for a job, your profile is not an acceptable place to make your profile 100 percent about you and your accomplishments. It is not a super-duper resume. It should be written so that the reader may get a clear sense of how you may help her. Think of it kind of like your personal introduction and fifteen-second commercial. Make it about the reader, and write it so that she will contact you.

LinkedIn provides you with an excellent venue in which to market your services and highlight your expertise.

Spend some time learning how to use LinkedIn most effectively. Use the tutorials that LinkedIn offers. Start by learning the fundamentals and go from there. Then use it every day. Like the old lottery ad proclaimed, *you have to be in it to win it*. You must use LinkedIn to get the most out of it.

Just like going to the gym once a month isn't going to make much of a difference to your body, dabbling on LinkedIn once a month isn't going to do much for your business. Visit LinkedIn every day, like you check your e-mail every day.

Investing ten to twenty minutes a day on LinkedIn, with time and commitment, will produce amazing results. I teach attorneys ways in which LinkedIn may help their practice and their profits, but at the end of the day, it's still up to them. You would think that all attorneys would be climbing on board.

By using LinkedIn regularly, you convey to your prospects that you are an attorney who is keeping up with the changing times. Perception is reality. How your prospective clients view you is critical. You have complete control over your profile and your online presence.

I stress to my clients that it makes no sense to set up a LinkedIn profile and then never use it. This is a waste of your cherished and limited time. If you want to make a bigger impact, increase your influence, and realize more income, you must schedule time for regular LinkedIn workouts.

Set up your LinkedIn profile if you do not already have one. Invest the time to complete your full profile. Go all-in and fashion a profile that makes you stand out, not blend in.

I will lean on the horn again here. Your profile should be about how you may help prospective clients versus being a resume of all of your accomplishments.

Get your social media fire started. I tell my clients to keep the social media fire lit, and as it burns brightly, all they need to do is throw a log on it every day to keep it stoked. You will never have to start from scratch ever again as long as you keep the fire burning.

In the beginning, social media is time-consuming, but do not let this deter you. Spend time each day developing your LinkedIn presence. Investing ten to twenty minutes a day interacting on LinkedIn is all you need to move the needle. I spend twenty minutes in the morning and twenty minutes in the afternoon. Start now. Don't wait. Every day that you do not use social media is hurting your practice.

The Last Piece Of The LinkedIn Pie

After you have completed your profile, try these three easy steps:

1. **Re-connect with old business contacts.** Search for names on LinkedIn. Many people have lost touch with a good business contact. Perhaps someone has changed companies. LinkedIn provides a perfectly acceptable way to re-connect.

2. **Keep in touch with new and prospective clients.** Where do you keep all of those business cards that you have collected at networking events? Are they scattered around your office, thrown into an old shoebox, or wasting away in a plastic card holder? If so, you are doing yourself a disservice.

The best way to ensure that you will stay in touch with contacts is to connect with them on LinkedIn. You may keep the lines of communication open between visits, calls, and e-mails. Using LinkedIn is the strongest way to stay in front of the clients that you have now and the clients that you hope to have in the future.

3. **Connect with fellow members of the professional organizations with which you are associated.** Many organizations have also started LinkedIn groups. This is a fast and efficient way to connect with other members of these organizations to ask questions, exchange information, or get input.

The bonus reason for investing time on building a strong online presence is this. In the past, advertising and marketing took time and money, but they may now be done instantly, automatically, and at little cost. Your online message is available all the time. There's no denying the fact that online marketing is becoming more popular and more lucrative.

I can advise you to conform to the changes that social media brings, but I cannot force you to do this. I will let the marketplace do that for you. Eventually, external pressure exerted by the ever-present technology changes will force you to shift the way that you think.

By the time that those of you who resist these changes are forced to adapt to them, those of you who proactively decided to welcome them will be far, far ahead of the pack.

Chapter 26
Stop Spinning, Start Evolving

You are now at the point where you become the decision-maker. Will you make the commitment to implement what you have learned? Will you master the steps in the sales process? Will you be one of the attorneys who make enormous amounts of rain, not excuses?

Reading this book is not enough. Results come from the transfer of skills, meaning that to get real improvement, you must make a commitment to implement the new skills. You must make this business development process a part of who you are, every day, in every way. This takes a discipline and persistence that many people lack.

You have been provided with the tools that you need to join that elite group of attorneys. By making the commitment to become a top rainmaker, you will take the step of implementing the strategies outlined in this book, and I will have accomplished my goal in writing it.

Whether your goal is to build a larger practice or to re-shape your practice, new business development skills will enhance your ability to bring in the kind of clients you want. The more effectively you acquire primo clients, the greater control you have in building your practice into what you truly want it to be.

It is unfortunate that many attorneys who do not develop these skills end up with a practice that *happened to them* rather than a practice that *makes them happy*. It's never too late to change this.

The biggest thing that stops people from taking a giant leap forward and creating momentum is that they don't know where to start to get some traction. They are overwhelmed with how to make client and business development work for them.

I tell attorneys that once they get the fire started, it doesn't take a lot of work to keep it going. I also share that the solution is easier and cheaper than staying with the status quo. This means that it is far less expensive to fix what is broken than it is to allow their practice to continue bleeding.

Don't keep shoehorning yourself into a business model that doesn't factor in what you want and value. Don't keep negotiating with yourself to justify staying on the revenue roller coaster.

Building your practice may be done by investing a limited amount of time each day. And yet most people don't do it. Not regularly, anyway. They resist. They make excuses. Or they start something new, and in a few weeks they start something else. They promise themselves that they will get started next month or next year.

It's not like they dig their heels in and shout, *I think I am going to run my practice into the ground*. They don't have to voice those words because their actions demonstrate it all.

I understand. I fought that demon when I was building my business. Even when things were tough, and I had to make it work, I didn't do everything that I knew I should be doing. I admit it. I was scared. I was unsure of my next best move. I knew that I needed to ask for help, enlist someone to hold my hand, walk me through the process, talk me down from the ledge. You may need that too.

So let me ask you this: Would you be willing to take a different approach? Would you be willing to stop following the masses and discover a process that you could use for the life of your practice? What if you stopped saying the same thing as your competitors and used your own unique language?

No one can force you into action. No one can move your feet for you. You, and only you, may make the change and produce results. You! Don't waste another moment not taking action. Be responsible for your life.

Nothing happens until you act. Nothing in this book will work for you unless you make the bold choice to take action. Success will be impossible unless you add a massive dose of action.

Below is some insight from author Andy Andrews:

I am a person of action. I am daring. I am courageous. Fear no longer has a place in my life. For too long, fear has outweighed my desire to make things better for my family. Never again! I have exposed fear as a vapor, an imposter that never had any power over me in the first place! I don't fear opinion, gossip, or idle chatter, for all are the same to me. I do not fear failure. For in my life, failure is a myth. Failure only exists for the person that quits.

Think about how many deals or how much money you lost this year because you didn't have a process that you could rely on over and over. Maybe tens of thousands. Lucky for you, my coaching programs cost nowhere near that.

If you are at the point where good enough is not enough, you have to act. But you don't have to act alone.

If you are going to do the work, wouldn't you rather learn how to do it the right way? I assist and support attorneys in getting the best results and getting ahead of the competition.

You don't have time to figure everything out on your own. Plus, going solo is the most expensive way to success. It costs you time and money, clients, and opportunities.

Every once in a while someone asks me if my coaching comes with a guarantee. We'd all like a guarantee before making a decision or taking a risk, but the irony is that taking the risk is what opens us up to our fortune. The reward only comes with the risk.

My guarantee is this. I guarantee that if you work with me you will have my undivided attention. You will have the benefit of insight and input that is relevant to your practice and personality. You will always get my highest and best thinking on any issue, question, problem, or challenge. I will show up to every meeting and every call on time and fully present for you. I make this promise to each of my clients.

I see attorneys misdiagnose themselves and wind up fixing their business development issues with something that usually doesn't address the problem. They listen to others tell them what to do because something worked for someone else in their practice. They try to be everywhere doing everything. That never works, and you wind up pulling your hair out and screeching things like, *I'm not getting anywhere! I am tapped out, stressed out, and maxed out! I'm spinning plates and running in circles!*

These attorneys have no clue what will work the best for their situation. When I am working with someone who feels stuck, we start out with three or four easy, adroit strategies and run like hell with them. Then we build on them.

If you want the future to be better than the present, you must take action now. To beat the status quo, you must have a goal and a purpose that is significant enough to initiate change, a reason that is compelling enough to make it worth the discomfort of changing, and the discipline and drive to see it all the way through.

Ask yourself this. *Am I moving in the direction in which I wish to go? Are my actions aligned with my goals?* If not, you may do one of two things. You may commit to taking action, or you may lower your goals and expectations and do nothing.

The interesting thing about not doing anything is that you will know exactly what tomorrow will look like, and the next day, and the next year, and the next decade. If you want comfort and certainty about the future, take a look at what you're committing to do today.

Those who thrive commit to taking action. They are all-in on every level. All-in means that there is no backing out. It means that there is no turning around. It's like deciding to dive into a pool. Once you decide to go all-in, you can't stop mid-air.

When you go all-in, you look at every activity. Every activity has a specific planned outcome. Your actions have a purpose, and that purpose produces results.

Making a change from where you are to where you want to go requires you to take action in that direction to generate momentum. Motivation gets you started, and habit keeps you going.

If you want help, maybe a little nudge, a gentle push, or a serious shove, I'm your gal. Let me assist you in being bold and brave, driven and decisive, committed and consistent.

If you want to have a continuous stream of clients and close more business, you must put some skin in the game and build a plan and a system that will help you in this endeavor. I am here for you.

Let's start a conversation. Call me if you have questions. If you are interested in finding out what working together would look like to accelerate your results, make a move. Dial the phone, tap out an e-mail, or send up a flare.

I hope that my words have touched, motivated, and inspired you to take some instantaneous and intentional action. Thank you for investing your time and allowing me to share what I was put on this planet to do.

About The Author

Liz Wendling is a Business Development Expert and Attorney Coach, who works with clients around the country and internationally. She is an avid golfer and spends much of her free time in the majestic Colorado mountains.

Liz's services are in demand by those who are tired of following the masses and who want to break away from the pack. She works with attorneys and other professionals who wish to take action and learn to achieve tremendous results.

In Liz's private coaching and training programs, she has assisted many individuals with the making of rain (and a hell of a lot of it!) in their professional lives.

Take the intrepid next step in being a wildly successful rainmaker. Learn the skills, tools, and tips that you need to achieve your goals. You are an e-mail or a phone call away from Liz. She is here to help you dash from mediocrity to fame and fortune! Discuss with her the program that works best for your individual practice.

Please feel free to e-mail Liz at liz@lizwendling.com or call her at 303-929-3886.

Please also feel free to let Liz know about a specific tool, strategy, or idea that you ran with that made the rain come down in buckets in your world.

CPSIA information can be obtained
at www.ICGtesting.com
Printed in the USA
FFHW021346101019
55502074-61293FF